ISBN 978-1-330-68121-3
PIBN 10091521

For support please visit www.forgottenbooks.com

1 MONTH OF
FREE
READING

at
www.ForgottenBooks.com

By purchasing this book you are
eligible for one month membership to
ForgottenBooks.com, giving you
unlimited access to our entire
collection of over 1,000,000 titles via
our web site and mobile apps.

To claim your free month visit:
www.forgottenbooks.com/free91521

English
Français
Deutsche
Italiano
Español
Português

www.forgottenbooks.com

Mythology Photography **Fiction**
Fishing Christianity **Art** Cooking
Essays Buddhism Freemasonry
Medicine **Biology** Music **Ancient
Egypt** Evolution Carpentry Physics
Dance Geology **Mathematics** Fitness
Shakespeare **Folklore** Yoga Marketing
Confidence Immortality Biographies
Poetry **Psychology** Witchcraft
Electronics Chemistry History **Law**
Accounting **Philosophy** Anthropology
Alchemy Drama Quantum Mechanics
Atheism Sexual Health **Ancient History**
Entrepreneurship Languages Sport
Paleontology Needlework Islam
Metaphysics Investment Archaeology
Parenting Statistics Criminology
Motivational

STUDIEN

ZUR

ENGLISCHEN PHILOLOGIE

HERAUSGEGEBEN

VON

LORENZ MORSBACH,

O. Ö. PROFESSOR AN DER UNIVERSITÄT GÖTTINGEN.

Heft III.

GEORGE J. TAMSON:

WORD-STRESS IN ENGLISH.

HALLE a. S.

MAX NIEMEYER.

1898.

WORD-STRESS IN ENGLISH:

A SHORT TREATISE

ON

THE ACCENTUATION OF WORDS IN MIDDLE-ENGLISH

AS COMPARED WITH THE STRESS IN
OLD AND MODERN ENGLISH

BY

GEORGE J. TAMSON, M. A., Ph. D.

LECTURER OF ENGLISH IN THE UNIVERSITY OF GÖTTINGEN.

HALLE a. S.
MAX NIEMEYER.
1898.

Preface.

The scope and arrangement of the present treatise are sufficiently explained in the Introduction.

I do not, by any means, claim to have exhausted my subject in these pages. Indeed, the field of investigation is a wide one, and I have explored only a comparatively small corner of it, although many more texts have, at least partly, been examined than those mentioned in the List of Works consulted.

The abbreviations used will be readily understood: they are those usually employed in works that deal with English philology.

Reference to any part of the treatise will be facilitated by the Table of Contents and the Index of Words.

Some difficulty was experienced in the use of technical terms, more especially in finding equivalent English expressions for the German "schwebende Betonung", "Taktumstellung", &c. I have usually placed the German, in brackets, after the English terms.

In conclusion I have to state my indebtedness, for the earlier part of my essay, to Prof. Morsbach's *Mittelenglische Grammatik*, and at the same time to express to him my thanks for valuable hints received from him during the progress of the work. Besides, the remarks on p. 107 to the end of Chapter II, are partly based on notes of his Lectures, especially the arrangement of polysyllabic nouns under various types.

Göttingen, March, 1898.

George J. Tamson.

List of Works consulted.

Texts.

The "Gest Hystoriale" of the *Destruction of Troy*. Edited by G. A. Panton and D. Donaldson. E.E.T.S. 39, 65. 1869 and 1874. (Usually quoted as *Troy-Book*).

Morte Arthure. Edited by E. Brock. E.E.T.S. 8. 1871.

The Vision of William concerning *Piers the Plowman*. Edited by W. W. Skeat. Oxford 1886.

Richard the Redeles. Edited by W. W. Skeat. Oxford 1886.

The Student's Chaucer. Edited by W. W. Skeat. Oxford 1895.

Gotfried's von Monmouth *Hist. Regum Britanniæ*. Herausgeg. von San Marte. Halle 1854.

Historia Trojana. Guidone de Columpna Authore. Coloniæ 1477.

Manipulus Vocabulorum, by Peter Levins (1570). Edited by H. B. Wheatley. E. E. T. S. 27. 1867.

The Royal Dictionary Abridged. By A. Boyer.[1]) Fourth Edition. London 1720.

Dictionarium Britannicum, or a Universal Etymological English Dictionary, by N. Bailey. Second Edit. London 1736.

Works that have been used for reference.

E. A. Abbot, *A Shaksperian Grammar*. London 1873.

H. Brandes, *Die me. Destruction of Troy und ihre Quelle*. Engl. Studien VIII, p. 179 sq.

---

[1]) The evidence for the accentuation of words as derived from Boyer's Dictionary is, perhaps, not of an entirely trustworthy nature. Boyer was a Frenchman, who came to England only at the age of about 20. Besides, the copy of his Dictionary, which we have used, is very badly printed, and the accents are not always distinctly marked. For particulars of the author's life, see the Dictionary of National Biography.

P. Branscheid, *Ueber die Quellen des Morte Arthure.* Anglia VIII, p. 179 sq.

B. ten Brink, *Chaucer's Sprache und Verskunst.* Leipzig 1884.

— *Geschichte der Englischen Litteratur.* Berlin und Strassburg 1877, 1893.

F. C. E. Elste, *Die Blankverse in den Dramen Geo. Chapman's* Halle 1892. (Dissertation).

G. Günther, *Ueber den Wortaccent bei Spenser.* Jena 1889. (Dissert.)

C. F. Koch, *Historische Grammatik der Englischen Sprache.* 2. Aufl. Kassel 1882.

G. König, *Der Vers in Shakspere's Dramen.* (Quellen und Forschungen, 61.) Strassburg 1888.

L. B. P. Kupka, *Ueber den dramatischen Vers Th. Dekkers.* Halle 1893. (Dissert.)

R. Lausche, *Ueber den epischen und dramatischen Blankvers bei William Wordsworth.* Halle 1896. (Dissert.)

J. Lawrence, *Chapters on Alliterative Verse.* London 1893. (Dissert.)

K. Luick, *Die englische Stabreimzeile im XIV., XV. und XVI. Jahrhundert.* Anglia XI.

M. E. Meiners, *Metrische Untersuchungen über den Dramatiker John Webster.* Halle 1893. (Dissert.)

L. Morsbach, *Mittelengl. Grammatik.* 1. Hälfte. Halle 1896.

J. A. H. Murray and H. Bradley, *A New English Dictionary.* Oxford 1884 sq.

H. Paul, *Grundriss der Germanischen Philologie.* Strassburg 1891—'93.

F. Rosenthal, *Die alliterierende englische langzeile im 14. jhd.* Anglia I.

J. Schipper, *Englische Metrik.* Bonn 1881—'87.

A. Schmidt, *Shakespeare Lexicon.* Berlin and London 1874—'75.

O. Schulz, *Ueber den Blankvers in den Dramen Th. Middleton's.* Halle 1892. (Dissert.)

W. W. Skeat, *Principles of English Etymology.* Oxford 1887, 1891.

H. Sweet, *History of English Sounds.* Oxford 1888.

— *A New English Grammar.* Part I. Oxford 1892.

W. Wilke, *Metrische Untersuchungen zu B. Jonson.* Halle 1884. (Dissert.)

Errata.

P. 30, l. 10. For *Parleying* read *Parleyings.*

P. 31, l. 19. For *fórt-with* read *fórth-with.*

P. 54, l. 16. Dele *mysschap* and 7758.

P. 62, l. 8 from bottom. *For* pp. 61, 62 *read* p. 61.

P. 63, l. 2 from bottom. For *precinet* read *precinct.*

P. 63, last line. *For* Bei *read* In.

P. 71, l. 4. *For* 80 *read* 79.

P. 72, l. 2. Dele *emulator.*

P. 73, l. 16. For *lamentacoun* read *lámentacoun.*

P. 79, l. 8 from bottom. *For* 69 *read* 70.

P. 90, l. 7 from bottom. *déliuer* belongs to p. 102, 6 a).

P. 96, l. 12 from bottom. *éncombre* belongs to **p.** 102, 6 c).

P. 98, l. 9. *For* 71 *read* 70.

P. 112, l. 10. Dele *array (arrayen).*

P. 118. Dele line 14 and 15.

P. 121, l. 5. Dele *retenaunce.*

P. 129, l. 13. Dele *conster.*

Table of Contents.

Introduction.

The revival of alliterative poetry in the fourteenth century is one of the most remarkable features in the history of English literature. For the student of language this poetry is of special importance, because alliteration affords one of the principal criteria for ascertaining the accent of words. From this point of view the alliterative poems of that period have as yet been too little examined, and we possess hitherto no work or article in which this subject is comprehensively dealt with.

It will therefore be the object of the present investigation to examine carefully, especially in compounds, the word-stress in Middle English, as it may be deduced from the accentuation prevailing among our alliterative poets.

In this connection simple or uncompounded words need not be considered, as in such words, when they consist of more than one syllable, the chief stress in Middle English, in agreement with the practice in Old and in Modern English, is constantly laid on the first syllable, which is the root-syllable (cf. Morsbach, *Me. Gramm.* § 20).

Apart from *Richard the Redeles* three important works of considerable extent, of different dates, and by different authors, have been used as the basis of our investigation, viz. the so-called *Troy-Book*, the *Morte Arthure* and *Piers the Plowman*.

Considered from a metrical point of view, the first of these is undoubtedly the most important, owing to its superiority over the other poems, especially over *Piers the Plowman,* in respect to the care and accuracy with which the system of alliteration has been applied.

Although the following few observations concerning the authorship, the time of composition, and the dialect of our poems may contain nothing new, it will perhaps not be out of place, if we briefly recapitulate what is known in respect to these several matters.

The *Troy-Book*.

Various opinions have been expressed on the question of the authorship of this work. Donaldson, in the Preface to his edition of the *Troy-Book* for the E. E. T. S., advocates the view that the poet who wrote the *Morte Arthure* is also the author of the *Troy-Book*. He bases this opinion chiefly on the similarity of the vocabulary in both works, and says: „In both poems we find the same peculiar words and phrases, the same peculiarities of thought, the same favourite subjects, and the same methods of viewing and representing them: even the differences of thought and expression are such as could be presented only by the same mind in different moods.“

Morris, in the Preface to his edition of *Early English Alliterative Poems,* for the E. E. T. S., is inclined to see the author of the *Troy-Book* in the writer of those poems. He adduces the following reasons in support of this opinion: „... for, leaving out identical and by no means common expressions, we find the same power of description and the same tendency to inculcate moral and religious truths on all occasions where an opportunity presents itself.“

Remarks, somewhat vague and general in expression, like those quoted, are hardly convincing. A more accurate examination of this subject is found in Trautmanns article „*Der Dichter Huchown und seine Werke*“ (*Anglia* I p. 109 sq.). On the basis of metrical investigations, he reaches the conclusion that the *Morte Arthure* and the *Troy-Book* are not by the same hand. This question was afterwards again dealt with by Brandes in his essay „*Die me. Destruction of Troy und ihre Quelle*“ (*Engl. Studien* VIII p. 398 sq.). Against Trautmann he upholds the authorship of Huchown for our poem.

It would carry us beyond the scope of the present treatise to enter more fully into this question. We would, however, offer one more remark on the subject. When Wyntown, in *Þe Originale Cronykil of Scotland,* v. 304 sq. says of Huchown:

He made þe gret Gest of Arthure
And þe Awntyre of Gawane
Þe Pystyl als of Swete Swsane,

it may appear strange that, if Huchown were also the author
of the *Troy-Book*, Wyntown should have made no mention
whatever of this work, a poem both more extensive and
certainly not less important than those that are mentioned
by him.

Formerly the *Troy-Book* was assigned to the second half
of the fourteenth century. According to Kölbing (*Engl. Stud.*
XI 285), the poet of the *Troy-Book* clearly imitated Chaucer.
The poem must, therefore, be later, about the beginning of
the fifteenth century, and consequently cannot be ascribed, as
it has been, to Shir Hew of Eglintoun.

With reference to the dialect of the *Troy-Book*, Luick
(*Anglia* XI p. 406), says: „Consequently the *Troy-Book* will
probably belong to the northern part of the West-Midland".

Morte Arthure.

According to Trautmann (*Anglia* I, p. 109 sq.), Huchown
is probably to be accepted as the author of the *Morte Arthure*
(cf. also T. P. Harison: *A Study of the ME. Poem, The Pystal
of Susan.* Mod. Lang. Assoc. Publications, vol. VIII No. 4
Baltimore 1893; but also ten Brink, *Hist. of English Lit.* II,
p. 402 sq., and Luick, l. c. p. 586).

With reference to the time and locality of the composition
of the *Morte Arthure* ten Brink (l. c. p. 403) says: „The author
of this poem wrote probably in the north of England towards
the beginning of the fifteenth century". And Luick (l. c. p. 586):
„In any case our poem is not of Midland origin, but more
northern than all the documents which we have hitherto considered".

Piers the Plowman.

For this work we possess distinct data as to authorship
and time of composition. The facts in connection with these
points are generally known and accepted. The author of the
poem is William Langland (or Langley), who was born about
1331 in south Shropshire at Cleobury Mortimer situated between

Ludlow and Kidderminster, and who died about the year 1400. The poem is preserved in numerous MSS. in three different versions: the A-text 1362, the B-text 1377, and the C-text 1393.

As to the dialect of the work, Skeat (Clar. Press. edition, vol. II p. lvii.) gives his opinion as follows: „There can be little doubt that the true dialect of the author is best represented by MSS. of the B-text, and that this dialect was mainly Midland, with occasional introduction of Southern forms. The A-text was printed from the Vernon MS., as this seemed to be the best MS., upon the whole; none of the MSS. of that text being very satisfactory. But the Vernon MS. differs in dialect from almost all other copies of the poem; the scribe, who has written out a large number of other poems also, has turned everything into the Southern dialect. The MSS. of the C-text are mostly in a Midland dialect, but it is remarkable that many of them frequently introduce Western forms, as if the author's copy had been multiplied at a time when he had returned to the West of England". (cf. Morsbach, *Me. Gramm.* § 3 Anm. 2: „Also the so-called B-text of Langland's *Piers the Plowman* affords evidence of an altogether insufficient nature as to questions of dialect".) [1]

Richard the Redeles.

The poem of *Richard the Redeles*, so called by Skeat according to this expression in the first verse of Passus Primus:
Now, Richard the Redeles · reweth on ʒou-self,
consists of a *Prologus* of 87, and of four *Passus* respectively of 114, 192, 371, and 93 verses. Skeat (l. c. p. lxxxiii sq.) assigns it to the year 1399 and to the author of *Piers the Plowman.*

As we stated before, from a metrical point of view, the *Troy-Book* is the most important of our texts, because it is the most regular in the use of alliteration. As a rule there

---

[1] For the dialect of the B-text, see the dissertation of Kron, *Untersuchungen zu W. Langley* etc., Erlangen 1885. There (pp. 13, 27 sq. and p. 53) the MS. Laud Misc. 551 is stated to be in the poet's handwriting, which is distinctly denied by Morsbach (*Me. Gramm.* § 129 Anm. 8). Skeat also (p. lxviii) believes this MS. to be „the author's autograph copy".

are two accented words in the first and one in the second half of the verse. Only occasionally do we meet with verses containing merely one alliterative word in each half-verse, or with so-called „crossed alliteration" (cf. Lawrence, *Chapters on Allit. Verse,* p. 77).

Metrically the *Morte Arthure* is less correct than the *Troy-Book,* whereas the deviations from the identity of stressed and alliterative words are most frequent in *Piers the Plowman.* These facts are generally known, and will be confirmed and illustrated by the following investigation, which will, therefore, at the same time present a contribution, although a modest one, to the knowledge of the metrical composition of Middle English alliterative verse.

Chapter I.

We possess various means for ascertaining the word-stress in Middle English: 1. The language of the poets: rhythm, alliteration, rhyme. 2. Certain changes in the language: weakenings of sounds, syncope etc. 3. Conclusions drawn from Modern English, both from the accentuation of the present day, and from direct evidence of an earlier date, e. g. from the *Manipulus Vocabulorum* belonging to the sixteenth century (cf. Morsbach, *Me. Gramm.* § 18).

Among those different tests, we shall principally use that of alliteration, for, as Schipper (*Grundriss* II¹ p. 1038) puts it: „The supreme law for the connection between word-stress and metrical stress requires, in all verse based upon the principle of accent, that the latter should be in agreement with the former. This applies in an equal measure to the alliterative line and to „equipedal" verse („gleichtaktige Versarten")". Where in our texts this agreement is not found to exist, we shall have to decide by means of one or other of the criteria mentioned above, whether the accentuation in question can be justified or not.

We divide the material collected in the following pages into two principal groups, a *Germanic* or *English* and a *Romance* group. In the further subdivision of the former we follow the one adopted by Morsbach in his Middle English Grammar.

For reasons already referred to in the Introduction we base our conclusions in the cases that will come under discussion, in the first place on the *Troy-Book*.

A. The Germanic or English Element.[1])
I. Original Nominal Compounds and their Analogues.

a) In the *Troy-Book:*

árowsmythis, 1588.

bélmakers, 1589.

bélt stid, 5940.

bládsmythis, 1592.

bódword, bódeword, 6262, 8315.

búrgh-men, 8570.

éuensangtyme, 8919.

góldsmythes, 1584.

hérne-pon, 8775.

hórse fete, hórsfet, 5834, 6560.

léfs-ales, léfe-sals, 337, 1167. (Cf. Chaucer, *Reves T.: levesel*).

nightwácche, 7352:

> *Nightwacche for to wake, waites to blow,*

But also *skóute-wacche, skówte wacche*, 1089, 6042.

sópertyme, 3398.

fórward (= agreement), 548, 602, 636, 651, 704, 2440, 2727, 3123, 7985, 9312; (= vanguard) 1148, 5860.

The first part of the word has the chief stress, quite regularly. We find this accentuation already in OE. and likewise still in the Modern Dutch *vóorwaarde*.

fórwise, 2539, 3950.

áfterwarde, 121.

éftsones, 2478, 7245, 11518. (Cf. p. 16.)

áuerthwert, óuerthwert, 7532, 8348.

These also have the regular stress.

wanspede has the stress on the first syllable in v. 9327; in v. 7945 on the second:

> *My wonsped to aspie in dispite ay.*

If the rime-letters are here placed correctly in the first half verse, we must assume that the accentuation of this word was

---

[1]) In this division we also place words of Romance origin, when they are provided with a Germanic prefix, and formations like s o p e r - t y m e.

a shifting one. In OE. the syllable *wan-* (*won-*) was stressed, as it is still in Modern Dutch, e. g. *wánhoop, despair*

míshap, 2069, 13133.

mísrewle, mýsrewle, 6128, 7952.

In OE, in such compounds, the prefix *mis-* was regularly stressed. In ME. the accentuation varies (cf. Morsbach, § 24², and Anm. c.). In our texts we have discovered only one example of unstressed *mis-*: *myserúle, Rich. the Redeles, Pass.* 4, 3. In the *Manip. Vocab.* we find *misdéede* 52, 33, but *míshappe* 27, 27, and *mísrewle* 95, 44. In Mod. E. this prefix is unstressed, as in *mistáke, misháp*, or has a weak stress, as in *mìsdéed*. Sweet (*A New Engl. Gram.* § 919) says: „Some prefixes which have a very definite meaning and are phonetically capable of being detached from the body of a word have in consequence come to be felt as independent words, the prefix and the body of the word being balanced against one another, as it were, by each receiving equal stress", and quotes among his examples the word ·*mis·conduct* in which the dots indicate his accentuation. To me it seems more than doubtful that both parts of the word receive „equal stress", although certainly the prefix is not altogether unstressed.

Compounds with the negative particle *un-*, which in OE. had still mostly the chief stress on the first part, shift their accent in ME. In Mod. E. this prefix is usually unaccented, or has a secondary stress, as in *ùnbelíef* (cf. Sweet, *NE. Gram.* § 919, and Morsbach § 24² and Anm. a).

vnbest (= monster), 7766.

vnkýndness, 144, 1923.

vnpóssible, 258.

unstíthe, 117.

vncléne, 1639, 1845.

vnfáithful, 714.

vntrúly, 723.

b) in the *Morte Arthure*.

bále-fyre, 1048.

blód-hondes, 3640.

cáremane, 957. (Cf. Oxf. Dict.: *carman*.)

cópe-borde, 206. (Cf. Oxf. Dict.: *cupboard*.)

crósse-dayes, 3212.

dede-thráwe, 1150:

> The theeffe at the dede-thrawe so throly tyme thryngez

Cf. *Gamelyn* 24:

> On his deeþ bed to a-bide Goddes wille.

Here, perhaps, a shifting of accent took place (cf. Morsb. §§ 26, 27). In OE. the first part of the word had of course the chief stress (cf. *Béowulf* 2901)

dúle-cotes, 4336.

éuensange, éuesange, 894, 900.

eye-líddes, 3953:

> Lokes one his eye-liddis, that lowkkide ware faire.

Probably here also a shifting of accent may be assumed.

fáa-mene, 303.

fóte-mene, 1989.

hánnde-brede, 2229.

hánsemane, hánsemene, 2662, 2743. (In the Gloss. Index explained as *henchman, page*. Cf. Skeat, *Etym. Dict.: henchman*.)

hérne-pane, 2229.

kételle-hattes, kéttille-hatte, 2993, 3516, 3995.

mórne-while, 2001, 3223.

neke-bóne, 2771:

> And brustene his neke-bone, that alle his breste stoppede!

Here also, perhaps, a shifting of accent. Cf. Burns's *Tam o'Shanter*:

> Whare drunken Charlie brak's neck-bane.

scháft-monde, 2546, 3843, 4232.

schíppemene, 1212.

schírreues, 725.

schýnbawde, 3846.

tóppe-castelles, 3616.

wátyre-mene, 741.

wólfe-heuede, 1093.

fórchipe, 3678.

fóretoppe, 1078.

fórheuede, 1080.

fórestayne, 742.

fórtethe, 1089, but

forsterne, 3664:

> *So stowttly the forsterne one the stam hyttis,*

or should we perhaps assume that the first half-verse contains only one rime-letter and in that case accentuate *fórsterne?*
fró warde, 3345.
sélcouthe, sélkouthe, sélkouthely, 75, 1298, 1948, 3252, 3531.
in-come, 2009, but
in-cóme, 2171:

> *Bot Kayous at the in-come was kepyd vn-fayre.*

A case analogous to that of *forsterne.*
óuer-hande, 4300.
óuerlynge, 289, 520, 710.
ówte-iles, ówt illes, 30, 2359.
ówte-mowntes, 3909.
ówte landes, owt londes, 2607, 2723, but
owt-lóñdys, 3697:

> *When ledys of owt-loñdys leppyne in waters,*

again a case analogous to those above.
incouthe, 3449, but
vncówthe, 3514:

> *And that castelle es cawghte with vncowthe ledys.*

With accented *un-* the word occurs also in Chaucer (Koch I, S. 161):

> *So uncouth and so riche, and wroght so weel (Kn. T.* 1639),

in Spenser (Günther, S. 31):

> *In some straunge habit, after uncouth wize* (513b)
> *And doubtfully dismayd through that so uncouth sight* (328b),

in Marlowe (Bullen's edition):

> *An uncouth pain torments my grieved soul* (I, 45),

in Shakspere (Schmidt, S. 1415):

> *And thus begins: 'What uncouth ill event'* (*Luc.* 1598),

in Jonson (Wilke, S. 44):

> *May be our rise. It is no uncouth thing* (I, 404).

In the modern literary language we find only *uncóuth,* but the modern dialects lay the stress on the first syllable, because, in consequence of the special development of meaning, the force of the word as a compound was no longer felt. Cf. Morsbach, *Me. Gram.* § 26 p. 67.

unfáire, 303.
vnblýthely, 1434.
vnfáye, 2796.
vnférs, 4122.
vnfrély, 780.
vn-lórdly, vnlórdlyeste, 1267, 1313.
vn-méte, 4070.
vn-résonable, 3452.
vnrýghtwyslye, 329.
vnsékyrly, 966.
vn-sémly, 1044.
vn-slély, 979.
vn-sównde, 3290, 3931, 3942.
vn-spárely, vn-spáryly, 235, 3160.
vn-ténderly, vn-téndirly, 1144, 2575.
vn-tréwe, vn-tréwely, 886, 4227.
vnwíttyly, 3802.
vn̄-wýnly, vnwýnnly, 955, 1302, 1481, 3562.
vnwýse, 3317.

c) in *Piers the Plowman*.

Before proceeding to the examination of the examples from
Langland's poem, we must once more emphasise the fact that
he uses alliteration in a very free and irregular manner, and
that we have therefore to practise special caution in deducing
rules for the accentuation of words from his work. Cf. also
p. 17 under *inwit*. Luick (*Anglia* XI p. 430) pronounces, on
this point, the following opinion: „Langley's poem shows a
peculiar irregularity in the construction of his verse. At one
time his verse flows on quite smoothly and pleasantly, especially
at the end of the Passus, at another time we find such an
accumulation of unstressed syllables and so faulty a distribution
of accented ones, that the rhythm is almost entirely lost, and
many passages afford examples of the worst alliterative verse
of the fourteenth century (on the treatment of Alliteration cf.
also Bühlbring, *Anglia*, Beiblatt VII). Moreover, the placing
of the rime-letters is often unsatisfactory or faulty: they fall on
syllables, that have no verbal or syntactic stress, nay more,
they are often entirely absent“. Skeat also (Clar. Press Edit.

vol. II p. lxi) gives an equally unfavourable verdict on the poet's metrical practice: „...Langland was not very particular about his metre. He frequently neglects to observe the strict rules, and evidently considered metre of much less importance than the sense".

We shall now illustrate those remarks more fully by a few examples.

As in the following verse:

He schólde not be só hardi· to decéyue so the péple (A. Pr. 76)

we frequently find an unstressed syllable provided with the alliteration. It would seem that L. himself was not satisfied with this verse, for in the B-text it appears in the form:

His seel shulde nouȝt be sent· to deceyue the peple.

An improvement in the later texts is also found in:

Bot the parisch prest and he· departed the seluer (A. Pr. 78).

for which we have in B:

For the parisch prest and the pardoner· parten the siluer

and in C:

The parsheprest and the pardoner· parten the seluer.

In the following verse the alliteration of the first half-line is not carried on into the second, which has instead an alliteration of its own:

Ȝoure gráce and ȝoure góod happe· ȝoure wélthe for to wýnne (A 1, 176).

This verse is not found in B and C.

In B Prol. 180:

And helden hem vnhardy· and here conseille feble.

the chief-letter is found at the beginning of an unstressed word.

In A 1, 11:

And seide, 'merci, madame· what is this to mene?'

the chief-letter begins the latter of the two strong syllables in the second half-line.

The alliteration fails altogether in:

That one is vesture· from chele the to saue (B I, 23).

Cases like the preceding ones show sufficiently that L. does not bestow much care on his metre. Further proofs of this negligence will be found in the discussion of the following examples.

When these occur in all the three texts, we quote from A; when they are wanting in A, we take them from B, and from C when neither A nor B contains the example.

bátte-nelde, C 7, 218 (*pák-neelde,* A 5, 126).

bódyhalf, B 13, 317.

chírityme, B 5, 161.

colplontes, A 7, 273:

> *Bot I haue porettes and percyl· and moni colplontes.*

Here we have probably to assume that the chief rime-letter is wanting and to accentuate the first part of the word.

dáy-sterre, A 6, 83.

dóre-nayl, A 1, 161.

dóre-tre, B 1, 185.

éize-siht, A 10, 52.

fénel-seed, A 5, 156.

férthing-worth, A 5, 156.

féste-dayes, C 6, 30.

gléo-mon, A 11, 110.

lýnne-seed,
lík-seed, } C 13, 190.
lénte-seed,

lónde-biggere, } A 11, 209.
lóue-dayes,

lýf-holynesse, C 6, 80; C 22, 111.

méeltyme, C 8, 133.

móot-halle, B 4, 135.

múlle-stones, C 21, 295.

pény-ale, } B 5, 220.
pódyng-ale,

plómtres, A 5, 16.

rúgge-bones, A 5, 193.

shípmen, B 15, 354, 361.

sómer-tyme, B 15, 94.

sýde-borde, B 13, 36.

sýde-table, B 12, 200; C 16, 42.

wómbe-cloutes, B 13, 63.

bí-gurdeles, A 9, 79 has the correct stress (cf. Morsbach § 23, 1, Anm. 1). So also:

bísmeres, B 19, 289.

býlyue, C 2, 18 *bý-lyue,* C 6, 21 (livelihood).

by-heste, C 21, 322:
And dudest hem breke here buxomnesse· thorw false by-heste.

The prefix *bi-* had already usually lost its accent in OE. But we still find cases where it was stressed both in OE. and in ME. Cf. Morsbach, *Me. Gram.* § 23, and Anm. 1, where among the examples of original prefix-stress the word *beheste* is also quoted.

In all the other passages in *P. P.* where this word occurs, it is always found as here, at the end of the verse (A 3, 122; B 11, 60; C 11, 250; C 19, 123), once (C. 23, 118) at the end of the first halfverse, and *bi-* is always unstressed. Only in the verse quoted the idea might be suggested to make the prefix *bi-* the bearer of the alliteration, but more probably we have to assume that the rime-letter is placed irregularly in the second half verse.

forbóde, B 15, 570:
Aren férme as in the fáith· goddes fórbode élles.

Here also the rhythm seems to require the accentuation *fórbod.* But in C 4, 138 *for-* does not bear the alliteration.

fóre-sleuys, A 5, 64.

mán-kynde, C 11, 246, cf. also Shakspere (König 1, 65):
To the whole race of mankind, high or low (Tim. IV. 1, 40);
Thou common whore of mankind, that put'st odds. (Tim. IV. 3, 42).

ésteward, éstwarde, C 1, 14; C 2, 133.

sélcouth, sélcouthe, sélcouthes, sélkouthes, C 1, 5; B 11, 355;
B 12, 133; B 15, 579; C 19, 148.

fóreward, (= agreement), A 4, 13; A 7, 38; *fórward,* B 11, 63;
(= foremost) A 10, 127.

All these have the regular old accentuation.

afterwarde, C 18, 62:
And afterwarde awaite· hoo hath moost neede.

This verse again is metrically defective, as the chief-letter is wanting. We cannot, therefore, prove the accentuation *afterwárde* from it.

In B 16, 169:
Estwarde and westwarde· I awayted after faste

the (first) rime-letter, as is often the case in Langland, is placed on an unstressed or weakly accented syllable. We have, therefore, to accentuate *éstwarde*.

éuensong, A 5, 235.

In A 5, 190:

> *And seeten so til euensong· and songen sum while,*

we should accentuate *éuensòng*, a case analogous to the preceding one.

Compounds with *arch-*, which in Mod. E. have level stress, are accented on the first syllable in *P. P.*:

érchebischopes, B 15, 239.

érchedekenes, B 2, 173 aber

erchedékenes, A. Pr. 92 (cf. Morsbach § 24, 2).

„The accentuation *árchbishóp* is far more frequent in Shakspere than the modern *archbíshop*" (König p. 66).

In Spenser (Günther p. 36):

> *To Deanes, to Archdeacons, to Commissaries* (516 b).

mísdede, mísdedes, mýsdedes, A 1, 142; A 3, 44; A 4, 77; A 5, 55; B 5, 487; C 7, 274; B 10, 371; B 11, 131; B 12, 113; B 13, 386; B 16, 242.

mýs-hap, míshappes, mýs-happes, C 6, 34; A 8, 79; C 13, 201.

mýs-proud, mýs-proude, C 8, 96; B 13, 436.

ínstedefast, C 4, 390.

vncómely, B 9, 160.

vnbúxome, vnbúxum, B 2, 82; C 7, 16, 17; A 9, 93.

vncrístene, B 1, 93; B 10, 350; B 11, 138.

vndéuoutlyche, B Pr. 98.

vn-grácios, A 10, 206.

vnhárdy, B Pr. 180; B 18, 83.

vnhénde, B 20, 185; C 20, 249.

vnkóuth, B 7, 155.

vn-kuýnde, vnkuýndeliche, vnkuýndenesse, vnkýnde, vnkýndely, vnkýndenesse, A 1, 66; B 1, 19; A 3, 28; C 4, 264; B 5, 276, 437; A 10, 177; B 13, 219, 379; C 15, 19; B 17, 249, 250, 255, 342.

vnlófsom, vnlóueliche, vnlóveli, A 5, 207; C 11, 262; C 15, 179.

vnméeble, vnmóebles, B 3, 267; C 11, 186.

vnpácient, C 7, 210.

vnpárfit, C 7, 119.

vnpóssible, A 11, 225.

vnrédy, B 13, 216.

vnriʒtfully, vnrýghtful, C 13, 18; B 19, 239.

vnsáuvourely, B 13, 43.

vnskílful, C 7, 25.

vntýdy, C 4, 87; C 10, 262; B 20, 118.

vntréwe, C 1, 89.

vn-týme, A 10, 196.

vnwíttily, A 3, 101.

For these compounds with *mis-* and *un-* cf. the remarks above under a) and b).

Under this division we may also class the verbal adjective with the negative particle *un-*:

vn-héled, vnhíled, B 14, 232; B 17, 319.

eftsónes, B 19, 5:

> *I fel eftsónes a-slépe· and sódeynly me métte.*

In OE. the first part of this word was stressed, in ME. probably, as a rule, the second syllable (cf. Oxf. Dict. s. v.). Cf. also Chaucer:

> *And to the chanoun he profred eftsone (Chan. Yem. T. 735).*
> *Lest hit be hent eft-sones, so sat she (Leg. of Phil. 95).*

Cf. also p. 13.

euene-crístene, euene-crýstene, B 5, 440; B 17, 250, 260 is quoted
    in the Oxf. Dict. with level stress

ouer-plénte, C 13, 234:

> *Ouer-plente pryde norssheth· ther pouerte destrueth hit.*

This is the only example of the word in our texts.

éleuene, élleuene, énleue, A 2, 204; A 3, 174; C 10, 315; C 13, 174.

Here the Old Germanic accentuation has been preserved, cf. *Hêliand* 3423:

> *an thia elliftun tíd, thuo gêng thâr áband tuo*

and *Andreas,* 664:

> *nemne ellefne ōrettmæczas.*

For the shifting of the stress in this word cf. Morsbach § 27. The forms in Mod. HG., Dutch, and Swedish point to the old accentuation.

wánhope, B 2, 99; A 5, 225; B 20, 159; but

wanhópe, B 17, 309.

welcóme, B 20, 354:

'Thow art welcome', quod Conscience· 'canstow hele the syke?'

Similarly in Shakspere (Abbot, p. 391):

Nor friends nor foes, to me welcome you are (R.² II, 3, 170).

But verses like the following afford no proof for the accentuation:

Welcome, dear Proteus! Mistress, I beseech you (T. G. II, 4, 100) and in Marlowe

Welcome, renowmed Persian to us all (I, 26).

Owing to the position of the word at the beginning of the verse, we must, in the last two examples, read with so-called „Schwebende Betonung“, or „hovering stress“. Cf. also Morsbach § 114 Anm. 6: „In the frequent form *wĕlcome* (already in Laȝam. B) for *wilcome* (*wulcume, wolcome*), owing to a popular misunderstanding of the meaning, *wil-* has been replaced by *wĕl-*.“

Skeat (*Etym. Dict.* s. v.): „Distinct from A. S. *wilcuma*, one who comes at another's pleasure“.

inwít, inwítt, C 7, 421; A 10, 17, 42; C 11, 174; B 15, 546.

The word is found in L. only with this accentuation, unless B 13, 289 forms an exception:

With inwit and with outwitt· ymagenen and studye.

But the curious alliteration of *w* with *m* seems to occur also in other places, viz. in A 8, 42; B 13, 226; B 13, 359 (?); B 14, 137; B 17, 18; B 20, 111 (?); B 20, 186. Also *R. R.* 3, 348. In OE. the word does not occur in the sense it has here, and is probably an imitation of the French *conscience* with the same stress.

d) in *Richard the Redeles*:

héed-dere, 2, 117.

réyne-bowe, 3, 248.

mýsdede, mýssdedis, mýssededis, Pr. 38; 1, 59, 69.

myserúle, 4, 3.

Cf. the remarks on p. 8.

The examples of original verbal compound, which we have discussed so far, show that, generally speaking, the OE. accentuation has passed on through ME. into Mod. E.

The numerous examples in our texts of compounds consisting of two substantives nearly all show the old accentuation, which, in general, has been preserved in ME. and Mod. E., that is to say, they have the chief stress on the first part (cf. Morsbach § 22 sq. and Sweet, *New Engl. Gram.* § 896 sq.) We had to record only the following exceptions to this rule: *night-wácche, colplóntes, dede-thráwe, eye-líddis, neke-bóne, euensóng.* Of these only one (*night-wacche*) occurs in the *Troy-Book*, three (*dede-thrawe, eye-liddis, neke-bone*) are found in the *Morte Arthure*, and two (*colplontes, euensong*) in *P. P.* In the first place it should be observed that a close examination of the „Types", does not enable us to fix the accentuation of these words with certainty, as the types are in ME. less clearly defined, and it is therefore possible to interpret them in different ways. Occasionally, however, rhythm affords a proof for the stress, as for example in *P. P.* A 5, 190 (p. 14), where we are forced to assume Type A and defective alliteration. Now, the question is, have we to assume, in these few examples, a no doubt possible shifting of stress (cf. Morsbach § 22 sq.) or early instances of level stress? The latter alternative we cannot accept. Apart from the fact that Morsbach in his *Me. Gram.* (§ 26, 3) has made it highly probable that level stress appears only in modern times, the examples just quoted afford evidence directly against the assumption of an even accentuation, as words like *death-throe, eyelid, neckbone, nightwatch* do not show level stress even at the present day. On the other hand there is no reason why we should refuse to believe that the accent had been shifted from the first to the second member of the compound, on the principle that the meaning of the latter part received greater prominence than that of the former. Such shiftings of stress have been shown to exist already in OE. times (cf. Morsb. *Gram.* p. 51). Anyhow, the few instances in our texts of stress-shiftings, which are, besides, not positively certain, as compared with the numerous examples that prove the old rule, show that there can be no question of a wholesale shifting of accent in ME. times (cf. Kluge, *Grundriss* I p. 890; Luick, *Untersuchungen zur engl. Lautgeschichte* 1896, § 423), which is said to have been set aside again for the most part in Mod. E. That this stress-shifting, according to Luick l. c. was produced by French influence, is more than improbable, as on the contrary, words borrowed from the French gradually assumed the English accentuation in ME.

Man-kynde (p. 14) has still the old accentuation in *P. P.* In Mod. E. the stress has been shifted, and we pronounce *mankind.*

Euene-cristene (p. 16) is marked with level stress in the Oxf. Dict. The word is still found in Shakspere. In *P. P.* we have met with three examples of it, each time with stress on the second part.

Compounds with *arch-* occur only in *P. P.* where, with one exception (p. 15), the first member is accented. In Mod. E. we pronounce with level stress.

The single instance of *welcóme*, in *P. P.* hardly suffices to prove this accentuation.

In *eftsones* the stress varies in our texts: in the *Troy-Book* the first part of the word, in *P. P.* the second is accented. The latter accentuation was probably the usual one in ME. and is found also in Chaucer (pp. 7, 16).

Eleuene, which occurs only in *P. P.*, has still the OE. accent there (p. 16).

The single apparent accentuation *bý-heste* (p. 13) is also found only in *P. P.*, no doubt the result of defective alliteration (cf. the remark p. 13). The same applies to *forbode* (p. 14) and to *afterwarde* (p. 14).

In the *Morte Arthure* the second part of *forsterne* seems to be stressed (p. 9). But, as in the same text the particle *fore-* has the chief accent in five other noun-compounds, we may take *forstérne* as a metrical licence. The apparent accentuations *in-cóme, owt-lóndys* (p. 10) may be looked upon as parallel cases.

The stress of the particle *wan-* varies in the *Troy-Book* (p. 7). In the *Morte Arthure* we have found no example of this prefix, in *P. P.* only *wan-hope* (p. 16), three times with stress on *wan-*, once on *-hope*. In the other passages in which the word occurs (C 8, 81; C 12, 198; C 15, 118; B 20 165), the compound does not take part in the alliteration.

Inwit is found (five times) only in *P. P.*, each time with stress on the second part (p. 17 and the remark there).

The particle *mis-* (pp. 8, 15, 17) is always stressed in our texts, with only one exception. In Mod. E. it is unaccented, or has a weaker secondary stress. In the *Man. Voc.* the accentuation varies:

míshappe, 27, 27; *mísrewle,* 95, 44; but

misdéede, 52, 33.

The compounds with the negative particle *un-* (51 cases, some occurring several times) leave this prefix unaccented, with only two exceptions. That in *únbest* (p. 8) the particle has the stress, is explained by the fact that the word forms a strong contrast with the simple *best*, like the German *Untier* and *Tier*. Besides, *un-* is here compounded, not with an adj., as it is usually, but with a subst. Of *uncouthe* we had to record only two instances in *M. A.* (p. 10 and remark) and one in *P. P.* (p. 15). In the former text the accentuation varies, in *P. P.* the second part of the word is stressed. In Mod. E. *un-* is unaccented, or has a weak secondary accent, according to Sweet (*New Engl. Gram.* § 919) level stress. When we find in Browning (Edition in 17 vols. *Sordello* p. 147)

Of uncouth treasure from their sunless sleeps,

uncouth must be read with „hovering stress" („schwebende Betonung").

In a similar way *welcome* must be treated in verses like the following: Matthew Arnold (Macmillan's Edit. in 1 vol. *Sohrab and Rustum,* p. 72):

Welcome! these eyes could see no better sight,

and Tennyson (Macmillan's Edit. in 1 vol. *The Princess* p. 217):

Welcome, farewell, and welcome for the year.

These are simply cases of stress-shifting („Taktumstellung" i. e. the use of a trochee instead of an iambus). At the beginning of a verse and after the cæsura such apparent deviations afford no proof for the real accentuation.

II. Nominal Compounds of later Formation.

1. Substantive + Substantive.

a) in the *Troy-Book*:

kýnnesmen, 1734.

sóundismen, 8866 (cf. Stratm.-Bradl. *sande*).

b) in the *Morte Arthure*:

dógge-sone, dóggesone, 1072, 1723.

sándes-mane, sándismene, 266, 1419.

c) in *Piers the Plowman*:

dómes-man, B 19, 302.

All these have the regular accentuation: stress on the first part (cf. Morsbach § 29).

2. **Adjective (or Pronominal Adjective) + Substantive.**

a) in the *Troy-Book*:

álthing, 281.

sóche wise, 983.

súm tyme, 1729.

on allwíse, 5278, 10486.

súm wise, 12074.

any wíse, 12679.

„In OE., and likewise still in ME., in the majority of cases, the attributive adj. preceding the subst. has the stronger stress... As a rule *monŷ, all* and *ŏther* do not alliterate in ME., *fêle* rarely does... Likewise numerical expressions are seldom used as rime-words, also those that indicate quantity: *óld, grēet, smal, lŏng, diuers* &c." (Morsbach § 29). Cf. also Luick (*Anglia* XI, p. 396 sq.), who makes the following remark on the accentuation of the attributive adj.: „*Other* never bears the alliteration, and was probably unstressed." In the *Troy-Book*, however, we find it accented in the following passages: 1479, 1505, 2376, 2543, 3269, 4162, 7219, 7292 (*tother*), 11309 (*another*).

b) in *Piers the Plowman*:

other-gátes, A 10, 204.

otherwéys, A 6, 55.

other-whíle, other-whíles, otherwhýle, C 6, 50; C 7, 160; C 17, 364.

In Levins we find *otherwhyle,* 131, 20 without accent, but *sómewhile* 131, 19; and *otherwýse* 148, 27; *lykewíse* 148, 26. Cf. also Morsb. § 29 and the remarks under a) above.

alkín, alkýnnes, B 3, 224; B 6, 70 (Morsb. § 29).

In later times also the stress varies in such words, as we see from the *Man. Voc.*

alwáy, 196, 44.

nóway, 147, 9.

éveryway, 147, 8.

In verses like M. Arnold's (*Merope*, p. 356):

Always in arms, always in face of foes

we have of course to read the word with „hovering stress" („schwebende Betonung").

3. Pronoun + Pronominal Adverb.

In *Piers the Plowman*:

alsó, B 11, 302; C 13, 182.

„The OE. *eal swā* produces, in ME. with stressed *al-*, the forms *alsŏ* (but likewise *alsō* with stress on *-sō*), *alsĕ*, *als*, *as*, according to its meaning and function in the sentence" (Morsbach § 31).

4. Pronominal Adverb + Prepositional Adverb.

In the *Troy-Book*:

þerfóre, 222. 228.

Originally the prepositional adv. had the stress. In ME. the stress varies. (Cf. Morsb. § 32; also ten Brink § 280).

Verses like the following, from Chaucer and later poets, cannot be used, as they have been, to prove the real accentuation:

Therefore he was a pricasour aright. (*Prol.* 189.) Cf. Schipper
II, 137.

From Spenser (Günther, p. 29):

Provide therefore, ye Princes, whilst ye live (493 b),

Günther enumerates 21 additional examples from Spenser.

From Marlowe (but at the beginning of the verse):

Therefore in policy I think it good (I, 37).

Therefore in that your safeties and our own (I, 85).

Also in Mod. E. poets we find examples of such compounds, apparently with the stress on the. second part. These, however, do not entitle us to assume that those poets pronounced such words with that accentuation. So for example in Browning

(*Sordello*, p. 191):
Therefore he smiled. Beyond stretched garden-grounds.
(*Ferishtah's Fancies*, p. 32):
Wherefore should any evil hap to man.
In M. Arnold (*Balder Dead*, p. 134):
Therefore for the last time, O Balder, hail!
(*Merope*, p. 361):
A just, therefore a safe, supremacy.
In Tennyson (*Queen Mary*, pp. 593, 630):
Wherefore, ye will not brook that anyone.
Wherefore our Queen and Council at this time.

5. Prepositional Adverb + Preposition.

a) in the *Troy-Book*:

ítwith, 11753 (prep.), 11763 (adv.), 12201 (adv.). Cf. Morsb. § 35.

The stress in such words may probably have varied, according to their use as prepos. or as adv. As adv. they would often stand at the end of a sentence, or part of a sentence, with the stress on the second part.

b) in the *Morte Arthure*:

vn-tó, 4094.

The same accentuation in:
A graciose face to loke vnto (*Polit. Poems.* ed. Furnivall. p. 151).

In Mod. E. we accentuate *únto*, or with equally weak stress on the two parts.

c) in *Piers the Plowman*:

intíl, B. 13. 210.
intó, B. 13. 210.
vn-tíl, B. Pr. 227.

In these compounds the stress varies in ME. Now-a-days also we accentuate *ínto* but *upón*. Occasionally, however, we find, in Mod. E. poets, the unstressed syllable occupy the place of a metrical accent, so e. g. frequently the word *intó* in Browning, Arnold, and Tennyson. This apparent accentuation may be explained by the fact that in *into, upon* &c., especially in more deliberate utterance, both parts are stressed equally strongly or slightly. Examples:

In *Sordello* (p. 113):

> *That Language, — welding words into the crude*

Sohrab (p. 65):

> *But when the gray dawn stole into his tent.*

Queen Mary (p. 620):

> *Hath shock'd me back into the daylight truth.*

But stress-shifting („Taktumstellung") must be assumed in verses like:

Word upon word to meet a sudden flush (Sordello p. 143).
Brand upon temples while his fellows wore (ib. p. 263).

6. Preposition + Noun (or Pronoun).

a) in the *Troy-Book*:

belyue, 2525:

> *Brake sylense belyue, and abrode saide.*

Here we have to read with syncope *b(e)lýve* (Morsbach § 69) and to assume crossed alliteration.

withouten, 2775:

> *Wetys hit all wele: withouten any cause.*

Without as prep. has to be judged like *into, unto, intill, up(p)on* (Morsbach § 33). The two parts of these words were probably accentuated equally slightly in the sentence. In „equipedal" metre („gleichtaktiges Metrum"), for example in Elizabethan blank verse, we often find an apparent stress on the first syllable of *without.* This may be explained by the fact that the word was as a rule followed by a noun, that is, by a word whose first syllable was accented. Combinations like *without cause* &c. could be used in blank verse only when *without* was pronounced with „hovering stress" („schwebende Betonung"), which indeed approached most nearly to the actual pronunciation in this case.

The probability, therefore, of an accentuation *without* can hardly be established by the following examples from Elizab. blank verse.

It should also be considered whether the prepos. stands at the beginning of the verse or immediately after the cæsura, because in those cases no conclusion can be drawn as to the real stress. They would have to be looked upon as examples of so-called „Taktumstellung" or stress-shifting, a purely metrical device.

In Shaksp. (König, p. 67; Abbot, p. 338):
Eyes without feeling, feeling without sight (*H.* III. 4. 78).
I have cursed them without cause

      Now all the blessings (*Temp.* V. 1. 179).
That won you without blows! Despising (*Cor.* III. 3. 133).

In Chapman (Elste, p. 36):
For without your applause, wretched is he (46a).

In Webster (Meiners, p. 19):
(I speak it without flattery), turn your eyes (*D. M.* 65a).

In Dekker (Kupka, p. 16):
    Weares his apparell without appetite (II, 47)
with three other examples.

In Middleton (Schulz, p. 29):
To end me without words. Long may you live (I, 165)
and eight other examples.

In Spenser (Günther, p. 32):
    Man without understanding doth appeare (499a)
and 17 other examples.

In Jonson (Wilke, S. 43):
Against your mother's leave and without counsell (*M. L.* II. 53)
with three more examples.

amónges, 37.

Cf. Morsbach § 34.

b) in the *Morte Arthure*:

be-twýx, 801.
abóuenn, abówene, 564, 823.

    For these compounds cf. Morsbach § 34.

c) in *Piers the Plowman*:

abóute, BPr. 178; A. 8. 30; B. 13. 369; B. 15. 278.
    The verse last mentioned:
        Antony a dayes· aboute none-tyme,

presents a clear proof of Langland's carelessness in his metre.
We must assume either that there is no alliteration at all, or
take *Antony* and *aboute* (perhaps also *a dayes*) as the bearers
of it, for the word was never accented *áboute*, although apparent examples of it are given in the dissertations mentioned
above. A few of them may be quoted here.

From Webster (Meiners, p. 19):

Lurks about Milan: thou shalt shortly thither (*D. M.* 80a.)

From Middleton (Schulz, p. 27):

To bring my wishes about wondrous strangely (III, 598).

From Jonson (Wilke, p. 43):

What did he come for? About casting dollers (I, 664).

From these and similar passages we are by no means
allowed to deduce an accentuation *ábout*, which would be a
violation of all linguistic laws, also of those that obtain in
English. The prepos. should be judged like *into, unto, intill,*
u(p)pon, that have been dealt with before, and like *among,*
against, before, within, which we quote and discuss below.

amónge, amóng(us), A. 8. 79; B. 14. 237; B. 19. 420.

In the last of these verses:

At Auynoun, amonge the Juwes· cum sancto, sanctus eris, &c.
the alliteration is again defective.

In the following examples from later poets, we have of
course to assume „stress-shifting" („Taktumstellung"), or
hovering stress.

From Spenser (Günther, p. 19) *ámongst*:

Beg amongst those that beggers doo defie (514b).

From Shaksp. (König, p. 67):

And among three, to love the worst of all (*LLL.* III. 1. 197).
To make me blest or cursed'st among men (*M. V.* II. 1. 46).

From Webster (Meiners, p. 19) *amongst*:

Be worthily applauded amongst those (*W. D.* 20b).
These factions amongst great men, they are like (*D. M.* 81a).

From Chapman (Elste, p. 34):

This rule may hold well among common men (423b).

From Middleton (Schulz, p. 27):

Though among life's elections, that of virgin (I, 164)
and two other examples.

From Jonson (Wilke, p. 43) *amongst*.
Who amongst these delights would not forget (*V.* II. 265).
agáyne, aʒéyn, A. 11. 150; B. 18. 332; B. 19. 356; *aʒeines,*
    B. 18. 193:
        Adam afterward· aʒeines his defence.
Here the alliteration is given, as it often is by Langland,
to an unstressed syllable. Equally insufficient for proving the
accentuation *ágain* are the following Mod. E. examples:
From Shaksp. (König, p. 67):
We may as well push against Powle's, as stir 'em (*H.*[8] *V.* 4. 10).
That it is proof and bulwark against sense (*H.* III. 4. 38).
From Webster (Meiners, p. 19):
What's he? A lawyer that pleads against you (*W. D.* 20 a).
From Chapman (Elste, p. 34):
Shall back your murtherous valour against me (156 a)
with 9 others examples.
From Dekker (Kupka, p. 16):
Yes sure my stomack would goe against it (IV. 226).
From Middleton (Schulz, p. 27):
    That fellow will be roasted against supper (I. 200)
and 3 more examples.
From Jonson (Wilke, p. 43):
    I murmur against God for having ta'en (*V.* II. 259)
abróde, obróde, B. 14. 60; B. 5. 140.
abédde, B. 5. 395.
a-bóuen, C. 17. 35.
adóune, B. 10. 330.
a-fóte, A. 5. 6.
afýngred, afýngrid, B. 10. 59; C. 10. 85; A. 12. 59; C. 12. 50;
    B. 14. 162; C. 18. 67.
a-fúrst, a-fýrst, a-thúrst, B. 10. 59; C. 10. 85; B. 14. 162.
alóft, alófte, C. 1. 175; B. 12. 222; C. 21. 44.
a-mýdde, a-mýddes, C. 11. 67; C. 14. 43.
arést, B. 5. 234.
asóndry, B. 17. 164.
a-swíthe, A. 3. 96.
binéth, B. 16. 67.
bitwíxen, B. 5. 338.
to-fóre, B. 5. 457.

These are all accented correctly and present no difficulties (Morsbach § 34).

bifor, bifore, bi-foren, byfore, by-fore, A. 8. 39; B. 11. 303; C. 11.
179; B. 13. 440; B. 17. 104 (Adv.)

The last four verses present again examples of defective alliteration:

The bisshop shal be blamed· bifor god, as I leuc.
Of the blessyde baptiste· by-fore alle hus gustes.
Haue beggeres byfore hem· the whiche ben goddes ministrales.
Who is bihynde and who bifore· and who ben on hors.

The following examples again from later poets, in which *before* is placed at the beginning of the verse or immediately after the cæsura, cannot serve as proofs for the accentuation *béfore*:

From Shaksp. (König, p. 67):
Into the chantry by: there before him (Tw. N. IV. 3. 24).
That before you, and next unto high heaven (A. W. I. 3. 199).

From Spenser (Günther, p. 19):
That before God we may appeare more gay (517 a).

From Chapman (Elste, p. 34):
Ay, before him, I do not greatly care (54 b).

From Webster (Meiners, p. 19):
Who prefer blossoms before fruit that's mellow (W. D. 29 b).

From Jonson (Wilke, p. 43):
Two undertooke this morning before day (I, 734).

bi-hýnden, bihynde, A. 8. 93; B. 17. 104 (Adv.).

In the first of these verses:
And I bi-hynden hem bothe· bi-heold al the bulle
we have crossed alliteration.

The second verse has already been dealt with under *bifore*.

forsothe, A. 3. 66:
Here forsothe thei fongen· her mede forth-with
is a very badly constructed verse with defective alliteration.

with-inne, with-innen, with-ynne, A. 6. 37 (Adv.): C. 7. 31, 261
(Adv.); A. 11. 105 (Prep.).

We quote these verses:

With-innen and with-outen· i-wayted his profyt (also in B. and C.)
Other-wise than ich haue· with-ynne other with-oute.
The werst lay with-ynne· a gret wit ich let hit.

(B. 13. 363 has instead of this:
The worste with-in was· a gret witte I lete hit)
He hath wedded a wyf· with-inne this wikes sixe.

Here again the alliteration is repeatedly laid on an un-stressed syllable, while the last verse would be correct with alliteration of *wédded, wýf, wíkes.*

The following examples also from Elizabethan poets cannot be taken as proofs for the accentuation *wíthin:*

From Shaksp. (König, p. 67):
Ho! who is within there? saddle my horse (R.² V. 2. 74).

From Middleton (Schulz, p. 29):
Not within hearing think you? Within hearing (III, 297).

with-oute, withouten, A. 6. 37; B. 7. 55; C. 7. 31; A. 10. 57; A. 11, 164; B. 11. 251.

The first and third of these verses have been discussed above under *withinne.*

In the second verse:
That neuere shal wax ne wanye· with-oute god hym-selue.

either the unstressed *with-oute* has the alliteration, or the rime-letter is wanting in the second half-verse.

So also in the fourth und fifth verses:
And eke wantoun and wylde· withouten eny resoun.
And went forth on my wei· withouten more lettynge.

for which in B:
And went wiȝtlich awey· with-oute more lettynge.

The sixth verse shows parallel alliteration:
As on a walnot with-oute· is a bitter barke.

Cf. the remarks above pp. 24, 25, and the examples there quoted from poets of the sixteenth and seventeenth centuries.

In the combination of Preposition + Noun (or Pronoun) the word governed has of course the stress. Although in some of the examples we have quoted the prepos. apparently bears the alliteration, yet we cannot accept that it really was accented instead of the noun. The verses quoted before from a number of dissertations do not prove such an accentuation. Only a perfectly mechanical scansion will yield such a stress Poets of the present day, just as well as Shakspere &c., afford examples of cases in which an unstressed syllable would bear the accent by mechanical scansion, but no one could prove from this fact that such accentuations are or were ever heard in the the spoken language.

From modern poets we quote a few instances:

From Browning (*Parleying*):

Will without means and means in want of will (p. 167).
(At the beginning of the verse.)

Not without much Olympian glory, shapes (p. 201).
(At the beginning of the verse.)

With pity beyond pity: no, the word (S. 202).
(hovering stress.)

From Arnold (*Balder*):

From around Balder all the Heroes went (p. 103).
(At the beginning of the verse.)

So around Hermod swarm'd the twittering ghosts (p. 116).
(At the beginning of the verse.)

And before each the cooks who served them placed (p. 103).
(At the beginning of the verse.)

Crown'd, having honour among all the dead (p. 120).
(After the cæsura.)

Also in the following verses the preposition stands at the beginning of the verse:

(*Merope*):

Is without love or hate austerely raised (p. 358).
Stretch'd among briars and stones, the slow, black gore (p. 398).
Bent above all to pacify, to rule (p. 416).

From Tennyson (*Queen Mary*):

First beyond fall; however, in strange hours (p. 628).
Gone beyond him and mine own natural man (p. 640).

And after the cæsura in:

I have offended against heaven and earth (p. 631).

The number of such verses might easily be considerably

increased, but the examples quoted suffice to show that neither from them, nor from similar verses of earlier poets, any proof can be deduced for the real accentuation of those prepositions.

In Levins' *Man. Voc.* such words are not marked with an accent, with the exception of *ácross*, in which the accentuation is probably due to an oversight.

7. Some other Combinations.

a) in the *Troy-Book*:

éuermore, 3935, 4568, 6599. Cf. Morsbach § 35; also Oxf. Dict. s. v.: „In poetry the accentuation *évermore* sometimes occurs".

b) in the *Morte Arthure*:

alouer, 2027:

> *With egles alouer, enamelede of sable.*

Here the alliteration is *e, o, a*.

Cf. also Morsbach § 35: „The merely strengthening adv. *all*, the force of which is in many cases reduced to a minimum, never has the stress". We must, therefore, accentuate *alóuer*.

c) in *Piers the Plowman*:

fórt-with, A. 3. 66.

Cf. Morsbach § 35: „Also the strengthening *forth* in *forth right, forth with, forth mid* was probably unstressed as a rule".

On the other hand the strengthening word *euen- (em-)* always has the accent:

emforth, euene-forth, B. 13. 143; C. 16. 142; B. 17. 134; B. 19. 305.

Different again:

ouere-lónge, B. 11. 216; B 15. 235; B. 20. 358 with strengthening *ouere*.

III. Older and later Verbal Compounds.

1. Verbal Compounds with inseparable and unstressed Particles.

a) in the *Troy-Book*:

The following examples are stressed correctly with the accent on the verb:

abíde 171.

becóme 1712, 1714.

be-dághe 758.

begíle, be-gýle 612, 9279, 11197.

begónnen 1620.

beléft 13456.

beléue 4287.

belírt, be-lírten 715, 8134, 8447.

be-stád 5849.

betáght 6100, 11741.

betákes, betóke 1391, 5371.

bethóght 147.

betíd, betýde 2240, 2722, 2729, 9949.

betrát, betráut, betráutid 731, 11767, 12026.

by-flámede 888.

ffor-bóde, forbéde 5681, 5725.

for-bléd 12270.

for-jústede 296, 2088, 2134, 2908.

forsákes, for-sóke 630, 7071.

forshápe 13221.

for-wróght 5861.

for-yéten, for-yéton, forȝét, for-ȝéte, forȝéton 869, 882, 2068, 2291, 9959.

We have to record the following cases of doubtful accentuation in our texts:

ffor-bode 6428:

> *ffor-bode the firke þi fode forto wyn.*

It is better to assume here the absence of the first rime-letter, or deficient alliteration in the first half-verse, than to adopt the accentuation *ffór-bode*.

This applies perhaps also to:

forsec 721; and a similar explanation may be given for:

for-thinkes (= regrets) 9312:

> *And festyn in forward, þat him for-thinkes after.*

where we might assume that the rime-letter of the second half-verse is wanting.

In the following verses from later poets these words are placed again at the beginning or immediately after the cæsura:

From Shaksp. (König p. 71):
God forbid! Where's this girl? What, Juliet. (R. J. I, 3, 4).
God forbid any malice should prevail (2 H⁶ III, 2, 23).

From Middleton (Schulz p. 28):
I forbid all the sons of men to boast of (I, 182).

From Jonson (Wilke p. 44):
Of corne and victuall forbids longer stay (I, 756).

From Webster (Meiners p. 19):
That forsake falling houses, I would shift (D. M. 95 b).

b) in the *Morte Arthure*:

Also the following examples bear the correct accent:
be-cómmys 4317.
be-gýnnande 2963.
be-háldande 3107.
be-knówe 3867.
besékys, be-sóghte, be-sóughte 305, 1234, 1438, 3137.
be-tákyns 824.
be-tráppede 1630.
ffore-jústyde, for-júste 1398, 2895.
ffore-máglede 1534.
fforsétte, foresétt, for-sétt, for-sétte 1714, 1896, 1979, 2012, 2018,
      2161.
for-bríttenede 2273.
fore-brústene 2272.
fore-gýffe, for-géffene, for-gýffe 2184, 3483, 4324.
forelýtenede 254.
for-sáke, for-sákene 1686, 1945, 2734, 4142, 4182.
for-tródyne 2150.
to-rúscheez 1428.
to-stónayede 1436.
to-wrýthes 3920.

The remarks made under *forbode* and similar compounds,
apply also to:
forbere, 1913.
forsake, 1913, 2734:

34

I wille noghte feyne ne forbere, bot faythfully tellene.
ffore alle the fere of zone folke forsake salle I neuer!

vnbrýdilles, 2509.

vn-cléde, 4202.

vncóuerde, vncóuere, 739, 2710.

vndóne, 1722, 3752.

c) in *Piers the Plowman*:

The following compounds are correctly accented:

abíte, B 16, 26.

ablámed, A 5, 75.

ablýndeth, B 10, 264.

a-bóstede, A 7, 142.

abóuʒt, abóuʒte, a-búgge, abýe, abýgge, A 2, 95; A 3, 236; A 7, 152;
B 9, 142; B 10, 281; B 13, 376; C 17, 220; B 18, 401; C 21, 433.

abrýbeth, C 9, 246.

a-córse, a-córsed, BPr. 94; C 19, 224; C 21, 97.

adrádde, B 19, 21, 302; B 20, 350.

adréynt, C 23, 377.

a-férd, aférd, aférde, afére, a-féred, aféreth, A 1, 10; B 6, 123;
C 9, 179; C 16, 165; B 18, 120, 430; B 20, 165; C 20, 80.

affráyned, B 16, 274.

a-gást, agásteth, A 2, 187; B 14, 280; B 19, 295.

a-glótye, C 10, 76.

agón, B 9, 106.

a-lýghte, C 12, 144; C 20, 64; C 22, 202.

aquéncheth, aquéynt C 20, 251; C 21, 394.

aquýkye, C 21, 394.

aráte, aráted, B 11, 98, 367; B 14, 163.

a-schómed, A 5, 215.

a-thýnketh, C 7, 100.

awáite, awáyte, awáyted, awáytes(tow), A 2, 182; B 16, 169, 257;
C 18, 62.

a-wrék, a-wréke, awróke, A 5, 68; B 6, 204; A 7, 160; C 9, 158;
C 11, 288; C 18, 4.

bigíled, bigíleth, bigýle, by-gýle, by-gýled, by-gýlede, by-gýledest,
B 7, 70; B 11, 40; B 18, 230, 290, 337; C 20, 164; C 21, 166,
328, 329, 383.

bikénne, B 2, 49; B 8, 59.

biléeue, biléue, by-léouede, by-léyue, by-léyueth, A 8, 163; C 8, 74; B 10, 119, 232, 246; C 11, 167, 190; B 18, 257; C 22, 336.

bilóngeth, by-lóngeth, C 6, 66; B 10, 246, 359; B 16, 191.

bilóue, B 6, 230.

bi-lóure, A 8, 105.

bilówen, bilýeth, B 2, 22; A 5, 77; B 10, 22.

bimólen, B 14, 22.

bi-nóm, by-nýmen, C 4, 323; A 7, 228.

biquáshte, B 18, 246.

biquéthe, B 13, 10.

bi-séchen, bi·sóuʒten, A 2, 189; A 11, 98.

biséged, B 20, 214.

bisétt, bisétte, B 5, 266, 299.

bishétten, B 2, 213.

bisítten, A 2, 210; B 10, 361.

bislábered, B 5, 392.

bitít, B 11, 393.

by-gát, bygéte, C 2, 29; C 15, 31.

by-glósedest, C 21, 283.

by-hóueth, C 10, 89.

by-iápede, C 2, 63.

byschréwed, B 4, 168.

bysnéwed, B 15, 110.

by-swátte, B 13, 403.

by-tókened, C 19, 164.

by-tráuaile, C 9, 242.

by-túlye, C 9, 242.

bywícched, B 19, 151.

forbáre, B 3, 272.

forbéte, B 18, 35.

forbíteth, B 16, 35.

forbódene, A 3, 147.

fordíd, fordó, fordón, fordóne, A 5, 20; B 16, 166; B 18, 29, 42, 157, 343.

for-glótten, B 10, 81.

for-pýned, B 6, 157.

forsáke, forsáketh, B 5, 431; B 15, 82; C 18, 81.

forsháptc, B 17, 288.

forsláuthed, B 5, 445.

for-swóre, C 22, 372.

for-wálked, B 13, 204.

forwándred, BPr. 7.

forwény, B 5, 35.

forʒát, forʒéte, forʒéten, B 11, 59; B 17, 242, 331.

forʒéuen, forʒíue, A 3, 8; B 17, 242, 331.

to-bólle, B 5, 84.

to-bróke, to-bróken, A 8, 30; B 8, 87; C. 22, 346.

to-cléue, C 21, 114.

to-drýue, C 23 174.

to-grýnt, C 12, 62.

to-lógged, A 2, 192.

to-quáshte, C 21, 259.

to-rénde, B 10, 112.

to-réueth, to-róf, C 4, 203; C 21, 63.

be-flóbered, B 13, 401.

be-híhte, beo-híʒte, beo-hóte, bihýʒte, A 3, 30; A 5, 47, 235; B 18, 330.

beknówe, biknéwe, biknówe, biknówen, BPr. 204; A 5, 114; B 5, 200; B 10, 416; B 18, 24; B 19, 145.

be-léiʒe, belýe, B 5, 414; C 21, 358.

beméneth, by-méneth, BPr. 208; A 1, 1; B 15, 143.

beo-héold, APr. 13.

beo-lóuh, A 8, 105.

beréwe, by-réue, B 12, 250; C 19, 259.

bi-cóm, bicóme, bicómeth, bycóme, by-cómeth, A 3, 202; C 6, 61; A 11, 93; B 11, 195; B 19, 38; B 20, 378.

bifálle, bifél, by-fél, APr. 6, 62; B 5, 59, 479; B 7, 8; C 7, 326; A 10, 179; B 11, 286; B 16, 139.

bigán, by-gán, bygónnen, A 2, 59; C 2, 104; B 5, 295; B 18, 160, 210; C 20, 111.

We have to record the following cases from *P. P.,* in which apparently the prefix bears the stress. They afford again examples of defective alliteration or similar metrical negligences, and we are not surprised to find that such cases are most frequent in Langland's work:

bihelde, bi-heold, by-holdynge, A 8, 93; C 14, 134; B 15, 221.

The following verse from Middleton (Schulz. p. 28):

There's a stage — fig for you now. Behold all (IV, 345)
would yield the same apparent accentuation, with a mechanical
scansion, but affords no proof for the real stress of the word.

biseche, B 5, 510, C 7, 16:

> *Bydde and biseche· if it be thi wille* (also in C)
> *Haue ybe vnboxome· ich biseche god of mercy.*

In Middleton (Schulz, p. 27), but after the cæsura:

> *Let none of them see it, I beseech you* (II, 40).

bi-gonne, A 5, 189:

> *Bargeyns and beuerages· bi-gonne to aryse*

(also in C.)

In Shaksp. (König, p. 71):

And begin, 'Why to me?' Had she such power. (W. T. v. 1, 60).

In Middleton (Schulz, p. 27):

> *And begin all that ended long before* (I, 129)
> *Must beginn at the foot. Now, sir, who comes?* (I, 169).

In Jonson (Wilke, p. 43):

To beginne many workes, but finish none (St. N. II, 54).

All at the beginning of the verse.

bynome, B 3, 312:

> *His boste of his benefys· worth bynome hym after.*

by-trauaile, C 16, 210:

> *For no bred that ich by-trauaile· to bring byfore lordes.*

byȝute, C 3, 144 (= begotten):

> *And as a bastard ybore· byȝute was he neuere*

where A and B read: *of Belsabubbes kunne* in the second
half-verse.

for-bere, C 2, 99:

> *For thei shoulde nat faste· ne for-bere sherte.*

This verse again is no model of correct alliteration.

for-brende, for-brenne, C 4, 107, 125:

> *Fel a-doun, and for-brende· forth al the rewe*
> *That fur shal falle and for-brenne· al to blewe askes.*

In the second of these verses it would be better to assume
double alliteration: *fur, falle; -brenne, blewe.*

for-ȝete, forget, B 5, 404; C 8, 25; A 11, 285:

I haue made vowes fourty· and for-ʒete hem on the morne.
Vigilies and fastyng-dayes· ich can for-ʒete hem alle
And ʒet I forget ferthere· of fyue wyttis techinge.

The two first of these verses are defective in the alliteration of the second half-line, the third one in that of the first half-verse.

forsake, forsoke, for-soken, B 15, 35, 306, 496; C 16, 140; B 18, 194; B 20, 239; C 23, 38.

We will quote all these verses, in which apparently the prefix is accented:

And whan I flye fro the flesshe· and forsake the caroigne
for which in the C-text:
And when ich flee fro the body· and feye leue the caroygne.
Fonde thei that freres· wolde forsake her almesses.
How thei defouled her flessh· forsoke her owne wille.

Also in the C-text.

And a-vowe by-for god· and for-sake hit neuere.
Frette of that fruit· and forsoke, as it were,
And sithen freres forsoke· the felicite of erthe.

Also in the C-text.

Filosofres for-soken welthe· for thei wolde be neody
in which the alliteration is again very vague.

Cf. also p. 33

forʒif, forʒiue, B 17, 234, 287.

So wole the fader forʒif· folke of mylde hertes
'Veniaunce, veniaunce· forʒiue it be neuere.'

Alliteration of *v* with *f* occurs also elsewhere.

to-cleef, C 21, 62:

The wal of the temple to-cleef· euene a two peces.

For which in B:

The wal wagged and clef· and al the worlde quaued.

vnbókelede, B 20, 68.
vnbýnde, BPr. 101.
vnchárgeth, B 15, 338.
vn-dóth, vndóynge, vndúde, C 3, 40; C 10, 305; B 15, 589.
vn-fétere, A 3, 134.
vnfólde, vnfólden, vn-fóldyng, A 2, 58; B 17, 176, 182.
vn-héled, vnhíled, B 14, 232; B 17, 319.

vnknitteth, B 18, 213.

vnlóse, vnlósen, vn-lóseth, APr. 87; C 1, 162; B 17, 139; C 20, 114.
vnlóuke, vnlóuken, C 10, 143; B 12, 112; B 18, 187, 313.
vnpíked, B 13, 368.
vnpýnned, vnpýnneth, B 18, 261; B 20, 328.
vn-sóuwen, A 5, 48.
vnspére, vnspéred, B 18, 86, 259.

d) in *Richard the Redeles*:

Here we have only to record verbal compounds with regular stress:

a-góo, 3, 245.
aschónne, 2, 185.
awáyked, 3, 364.
be-léfte, 2, 30.
be-hóte, 4, 91.
beréued, 2, 137.
bicóme, 1, 49.
fforbéde, 3, 241, 277.
ffor-wéyned, 1, 27.

2. Nouns derived from Verbal Compounds with inseparable Prefixes.

These have the same stress as the verbs from which they are derived.

a) in the *Troy-Book*:

begynnyng, 2256, 2455, 4430.

In the first of these verses:

A blisfull begynnyng may boldly be said,

we have again to assume the absence of the second rime-letter. In the last two verses *begýnnyng* has the correct stress.

When we find occasionally in the correct verse of Chaucer apparent accentuations like *bíginning*, we have to look upon them as mere metrical licences. Cf. Morsb. § 47 Anm. 1, and ten Brink § 281.

b) in *Piers the Plowman*

forʒifnesse, forʒyucnesse, B 17, 221, 243.

In the first of these passages, the stress is correctly placed on -*ʒif*-; in the second verse:

> To the fader of heuene· forʒynenesse to haue

the chief-letter is wanting.

abýdynge, B 19, 289; C 19, 136; C 23, 142.

bileeue, A 6, 79:

> *Brutaget with the Bileeue· where-thorw we moten beo sauet.*

which is again a very bad verse.

The apparent deviations from the natural accentuation in the preceding sections, may be explained on the ground of defective alliteration, or of absence of a rime-letter. If we were to accept such deviations as representing the real stress of such words, the rhythm of the alliterative verse would, as a rule, become more defective, and the result would be types of verse, such as are otherwise not found in good poets. Such apparent deviations can, therefore, only be admitted at the expense of the metre. The majority of those faulty verses, as we have seen, occur in *Piers the Plowman*, which proves what was stated in the Introduction, namely that Langland by no means belongs to those poets that excel in form and metre.

As for the same apparent accentuations in Shakspere &c., they again may be explained by means of stress-shifting („Takt-umstellung"), or hovering stress („schwebende Betonung"). In poets of our own time also such examples occur. When, for instance, Browning (*Sordello,* p. 1υ2) writes:

> *Years ago, leagues at distance, when and where,*

we are, of course, not allowed to deduce from this verse that the poet, or anyone else, ever pronounced *ágo*. Besides, the word stands near the beginning of the verse, and we must lay the stress on *years* and -*go*.

3. Verbal Compounds with alternately stressed and partly inseparable Particles.

„When in OE. the full or concrete meaning of the particles, in connection with the verb, has been preserved, they have remained stressed and separable. When, on the other hand, by isolation of meaning, the particles are fused into a compound with the verb, they have lost the stress und have become inseparable."

„In ME. this applies also to those cases that present real verbal compounds. Many of the old combinations have died out, and other new ones have arisen" (Morsbach § 38).

a) in the *Troy-Book*:

With stressed particle:

óuerturne, 410, 12003:

> *The Elementes ouerturne, & the erthe qwake.*
> *Ilion to ouerturne angardly sone.*

We might also take the second rime-letter in each verse as wanting.

With unstressed particle:

with-drógh, with-dróghe, 920, 1224.
withstánd, withstóde, withstónd, 615, 3884, 4227, 5767, 10371.
ouercást, 13157.
ouerdrógh, ouerdróghe, 673, 4664, 7630, 9163, 11917.
ouerdrýve, 7068.
ouergrówen, 13457.
ouerpút, 160.
ouerráght, 69.
ouersét, ouerséttes, 3388, 3590, 3609, 12921.
ouer-túrnyt, ouertýrnet, ouertýrnit, ouertýrnyt, 1380, 1406, 3153, 4775, 7243, 7628.
ouerwált, 8155.
overcóme, 616.
underfónges, 266.

b) in the *Morte Arthure*:

ouer-chárggede, 1749.
ouer-fállene, ovyre-fállys, 1154, 3677.
ouergýlte, 207.
ouer-késte, 3932.
ouer-réche, ouerréchez, 921, 1508.
ouer-rédyne, 1415, 1524.
ouer-rónñe, 1206.
ouer-sétte, 2815, 4136.

ouer-swýngene, 1466.
ouer-whélme, 3261.
vmbecláppes, 1779.
vmbegríppede, vmbegríppys, 3758, 3944.
vmbeláppez, vmbeláppyde, 1819, 3785.

c) in *Piers the Plowman*:
With apparently stressed particle:
with-siggen, A 4, 142:
  That couthe warpen a word· to with-siggen Reson.
vnderfonge, C 17, 259:
  And haten harlotrie· and to vnderfonge the tythes.
The same alliteration *ha, ha, u* also A 4, 106.
vndernymeth, B 5, 115:
  Who-so vndernymeth me here-of. I hate hym dedly after.
With unstressed particle:
of-sénte, of-sént, A 2, 37; A 3, 96.
with-drów, with-drówe, B 18, 60; C 20, 62.
with-hált, with-héalde, A 2, 204; A 6, 42.
with-sítte, C 9, 202.
ouercám, ouercóme, B 10, 449; B 13, 11; C 21, 114.
ouer-cárk, C 4, 472.
ouer-clóseth, C 21, 140.
edwíte, B 5, 370.
ouerdón, C 14, 191.
ouere-láyde, C 13, 231.
ouere-réche, ouer-réche, C 8, 270; B 13, 374.
ouer-lép, ouerlépe, BPr. 150; C 21, 360.
ouer-máistrieth, B 4, 176.
ouer-sé, ouer-séye, ouer-séze, B 5, 378; A 7, 106; B 10, 328.
ouer-sópede, C 7, 429.
ouer-sprádde, B 19, 201.
ouer-táke, B 17, 82.
ouer-tílte, B 20, 53, 134.
ouertóurne, B 16, 131.
vnder-fónge, vndurfóng, vndurfónge, A 1, 74; C 4, 111; C 10, 129, 322; A 11, 171.
vndernóme, vnder-nŷm, B 11, 209; B 20, 50.
vnder-pízte, B 16, 23.

vnder-shóred, B 19, 47.
vnder-táke, C 1, 89.
vndir-wríten, A 11, 255.

d) in *Richard the Redeles*:
With unstressed particle:
ouere-gréwe, 3, 344.
ouere-lóked, 2, 35.
ouere-wácche, 3, 282.

4. Nouns derived from the Verbal Compounds in the preceding Section.

These also preserve the stress of the Verbals from which they are derived.

a) in the *Troy-Book*:
vndertáker, 3789.

b) in the *Morte Arthure*:
vndyrtakynge, 3187:
Of this vndyrtakynge ostage are comyne,
according to which we should apparently have to accentuate
vndyr-.

c) in *Piers the Plowman*:
ouer-skíppers, C 14, 123:
And ouer-skippers al-so· in the sauter seith Dauid.

The apparent deviations from the usual accentuation of verbal compounds with OE. alternately stressed and partly inseparable prefixes, occur nearly all of them again in Langland. It is, however, altogether improbable that he should have accented *únderfonge*, or that the poet of the *Morte Arthure* should have laid the stress on the prefix in *undyrtakynge*.

5. Verbal Compounds with stressed and separable Particles.

„Whereas in OE. these particles, when preceding the verb, were constantly stressed, we find that in ME. they have mostly lost the accent, when they were in closer combination with the verb; but not unfrequently the particle had the accent". (Morbach § 39).

a) in the *Troy-Book*:

With the particle stressed:
awáy lede, 377, 8607, 10963.
awáy past, 7819, 12832.
awáy toke, 6841, but
befóre past, 13301.
him bý stode, 9602.
dóun fell, 8617.
dóun lyght, 6990.
fór-sees, 2247:
    And for-sees not the fer end, what may falle after.
óutlawhit, 12373:
    And I, þat am outlawhit for euer of þis lond.
but *inwónes,* 133:
    All worshipped þat worthy inwones aboute. (Cf. 13863.)

With the verb accented:
away bórne, 666.
on to lóke, 1554.
vp dróghe, 755.
vp gráid, 1664.
vp sóght, 1091.
vp tíld, 1455, 1551.
vp wróght, 1542.

b) in the *Morte Arthure*:

With the verb accented:
abowte scho whírles, 3388.
ffurth he stálkis, 3466.

With the particle stressed:
a-bówtte rowes, 3629.
a-wáye passede, awáye passes, 3524, 3819, 3838.
awáye rydez, 3156.
dóune falles, 313; but

downe knélis, 3987, 3993.
fúrthe rydes, 2783; but
ffurthe stépes, 1213.

c) in *Piers the Plowman:*
fóre-tolde, A 11 165:
> *And fond as heo fore-tolde· and forth gon I wende.*

fórstalleth, A 4, 43:
> *Forstalleth my feire· fihteth in my chepynges.*
Also in B and C.

to-cómen, C 22, 243:
> *These to-comen to Conscience· and to Cristyne peuple.*

But for this in the B-text:
> *These two come to Conscience·*

Nouns derived from such verbs in *Piers the Plowman:*
forgóere, C 3, 198:
> *Ac gile was forgoere· to gyen al the puple*
but *fórgoers,* C 3, 61:
> *Forgoers and vytailers· and vokettus of the arches.*
So also in the B-text.

in-góynge, A 6, 117:
> *To gete in-goynge at that ʒat· bote grace beo the more.*

out-rýders, C 5, 116:
> *And religious out-ryders· reclused in here cloistres.*

For this in B:
> *And religious romares·*

vp-hólderes, vp-hólders, A 5, 168; C 13, 218
> *And of vp-holders an hep· erly bi the morwe.*

Also in B and C:
> *Up-holderes on the hul· shullen haue hit to selle.*

With the particle stressed:
a-bóute coden, A Pr. 40.
awéy stolen it, B 19, 151.
awéi renne, B Pr. 166.

a-dówn brynge, B 18, 29; but
adown brýnge, B 18, 35.
dóun brouȝte, B 18, 141.
dóun er he be taken, B 18, 70.
fórth gan me drawe, B 11, 41.
fórth gan I walke, B 13, 2.
fórth gan he wende, C 7, 352; A 11, 165.
fórth with hem he ȝede, B 19, 148.
fórth brouhte, C 3, 31.

d) in *Richard the Redeles*:

With the verb stressed:
oute that thei tóke, 3, 342.

This variety of stress in ME. in verbal compounds with separable particles, also shows itself still in early Mod. E. So we find in Levins: *fórecast*, 36, 10, *fóreiudge*, 183, 13, and *outláwe*. 45, 46. In Mod. E., when such combinations are still preserved, the verb has the accent, or we pronounce with level stress, according to Sweet.

6.

„When the particle follows the verb, the latter has, as a rule, the stronger stress, in OE. and in ME. It is true that in most cases a verbal object follows, or some other extension, when also Mod. E. has preserved the old accentuation. Yet these conditions do not seem to have exerted any influence in ME., as the verb, and not the particle, bears the alliteration, even without any further extension". (Morsb. § 39). Cf. also Luick (*Anglia* XI, p. 397 sq.).

Such combinations occur most frequently in the more vivid passages, in descriptions of battles and similar stirring events. Hence the examples are more numerous in the *Troy-Book* and in the *Morte Arthure* than in *Piers the Plowman*.

In the following quotations the term „Object" also includes „other extension".

a) in the *Troy-Book*:

α) Vérb + Part. + Obj.

back:
lokit báck, 6863: where the particle is stressed instead of the verb.

down:
báre don, 1210.
brént, & bétyn downe, 1730.
cást down, 1199.
gírdyn doun, 1377.

forth:
bróught forth. 692.
dráw furthe, 1137.
dróf forth, 498.
láuchet furthe, 1409.
pást furth, 812, 857.
séwid furthe, 361, 820.
shéw furth, 481, 522.
sílet furthe, 364, but
go fúrthe, 6132.

up:
brént vp, 889, 1379.
bráid vp, 904.
býld vp, 1535.
gírd vp, 854.
gríppit vp, 1377.
píght vp, 1578.
pílde vp, 903.
ríd vp, 1533.
sérchit up, 1534.
skrémyt up, 910.
stéppit vp, 351.
stáke vp, 893.
tóke vp, 1517.
wáckon vp, wácknet vp, 681, 2274.

wáynet vp, 676.
wént vp, 861.
wróght vp, 1552.

out:
gírde out, 177.
pás out, 568.
rút out, 912.
tílt out, 914.

β) Vérb + Obj. + Part.

after:
fólowet hom after, 1298.

away:
férke it away, 614.

between:
féll hom betwene, 1323.

down:
slógh hom downe. 1296.

forth:
léd hom furthe, 368

γ) Obj. + Vérb. + Part.

after:
hom séwet after, 440.

δ) Vérb + Part.

after:
to cúm after, 745.
séwet after, 1442.

away:
lúrkit away, 1369.

down:
góyng downe, 3072.
pút down, 1385, but
come dówn, 389, 504.

up:
stóken vp, 11.

b) in the *Morte Arthure*:

α) Vérb + Part. + Obj.

away:

rýdes awaye, 1418.

down:

bére doune, béris downe, 1486, 3736.

bétt downe, 2470, 3682.

chásse and chóppe doune, 2237.

chóppe doune, chóppede downne, 1406, 2368.

cráschede doune, 2114.

féllid doune, ffélis downe, 3345, 4087.

héwede downe, 4127.

knélis downe, 3951.

kýllyde doune, 101.

rýffes and rúysshes downe, 2913.

stráke downe, 2080.

swáppez doune, 1465.

forth:

bróghte forthe, brýngez furthe, 1381, 1483.

cárye forthe, 1165.

drífe forthe, 3276.

káyres furthe, 3996.

scháke furthe, 1213.

séndez furthe, 632.

stéris furth, 2923.

in:

cóme in, 176.

dráwes in, 622.

énters in, 1499.

fférkez in, 2071, 2802.

fféwters in, 2140.

ffíttez in, 2072.

gýrdez in, 2949.

kástes ine, 4243.

présses in, 2787.

rýdes in, 619.

sétt in, 1493.

slíppes in, 3923.

stówe in, 735.

swáppez in, 1129.
trússez in, 731.
trýnnys in, 3901.
túrne in, 583.

of, ofe (= *off*):
láched ofe, lághte of, 1515, 2693.
swáppes of, 4244.
tákene of, 2700.

on:
bráyedez one, 906, 1754.

out:
bráyd owtte, bráydez owt, 1172, 2069, 4215.
ffóundes owt, 4063.
háylede owtt, 2077.
láughte owtte, 2226.
pásses owte, 3913.
schótte owtte, 1705.
sénde owte, 1685.
swáppede owtte, 1795.
to wérpe owte, 9.

up:
búske vpe, 3072.
gáffe vp, 85.
kástys vpe, késte vp, 943, 3952.
káughte up, 3378, 4009.
láughte vp, 4183.
lókes vp, 4272.
pýke vp, 1636.
rýpe vp, 1877.
schóttis vpe, 3728.

β) Vérb + Obj. + Part.

against:
stóde theme agaynes 1489.

down:
chóppes them downe, 4261.
strýke theme doune, 561.

forth:
túrñes hym furthe, 3887.
lédde hyme furthe, 1515.
 in:
bróchis hym in, 4250.
 up:
káughte it vpe, 3995.
lífte me vp, 3349.
láughte hym vpe, 2292.

γ) Obj. + Vérb. + Part.

 down:
baneres he báre downne, 2212.
walles he wélte downe, 3152.

δ) Vérb + Part.

 down:
bráydene downe, 3945.
swéppene downe, 2508.
 out:
hénte owte, 2973.
sprénte owtte, 2062.
wéendes owtt, 2513.
 up:
cóuerd vp, 124, 957.

c) in *Piers the Plowman*:

α) Vérb + Part. + Obj.

 about:
príked a-boute, C 6, 160.
i-wríthen aboute, A 6, 9.
 after:
fólweth after, B 17, 80.
 away:
i-bóre a-wei, A 5, 89.
drýueth away, drýuen awey, B 9, 206; B 20, 173.
féccheth away, B 16, 45.
 down:
cóm a-doun, A 1, 4.

líʒte adown, B 17, 64.

pálleth adown, B 16, 51.

sprónge down, B 18, 86.

forth:

bríngeth forth, bróuʒten forth, brýnge forth, A 3, 147; C 7, 141;
 A 8, 76; A 10, 143; C 10, 260; A 11, 41; C 19, 102.

bóuweth forth, A 6, 56.

dríueth forth, A Pr. 103.

fólwc forth, B 11, 34.

fýndeth forth, A 11, 63.

lédeth forth, A 11, 20; B 18, 404.

plókked he forth, B 17, 10.

prófreth forth, B 17, 141.

prýked forth, B 20, 148.

púiteth forth, pútte forth, A 4, 64; A 6, 100.

rýd forth, A 11, 115.

sénte forth, B 19, 335; but

sente fórth, B 20, 80.

wénte forth, wénten forth, A Pr. 48; B 11, 164; A 12, 56; B. 15, 332.

in:

cóme in, B 19, 7.

of (= off):

cút of, A 4, 140.

gúrdeth of, A 2, 176.

on:

flápten on, A 7, 174.

out:

féllen out, B 1, 119.

kénnen out, B 17, 113.

púlte out, B 11, 157; B 15, 62.

ríde out, C 6, 158.

séken out, A 11, 187.

shéteth out, C 21, 294.

sóuʒte out, B 16, 108.

up:

arós vp, B 11, 430.

cówhede vp, A 5, 205.

rísen vp, rýscth vp, A Pr. 44; A 5, 176.

upward:
críʒinge vpward, A 5, 262.
túrned vpward, A 5, 19.

β) Vérb + Obj. + Part.

away:
lópe he so lihtliche awei, A 4, 93.
down:
I sát softeliche a-doun, A 5, 7.
pálte hym down, B 16, 30.
forth:
bár hem forth, B 16, 83.
léde hem forth, ládde hym so forth, B 17, 71, 117.
prófre it forth, B 17, 140.
pút hym forth, B 18, 40, but
ʒeue hem fórth, C 13, 165.

γ) Obj. + Verb + Párt.

forth, with the particle stressed:
the fruit that thei bringen fórth, A 10, 186.

δ) Vérb + Part.

down:
to bréke and to béte doune, B 18, 251.
forth:
cám forth, B 18, 73, 78.
gó we forth, A 12, 69.
rénne forth, B 16, 273.
trólled forth, B 18, 296.
dráwen forth, A 11, 30.
out:
lépen out, A 2, 207.
pút out, A 1, 116.
wént out, B 1, 122.
up:
lŏked vp, B Pr. 123.
rós vp, B 16, 226.
sprýngeth vp, C 14, 24.

d) in *Richard the Redeles*:

Vérb + Part.

cást adoun, 2, 52.
gáglide forth, 3, 101.
ytáke fforth, 3, 143.

7. Examples of Verbal Compounds with *mis-*.

"Since ancient times combinations with *mis-* and *full-* have
been in current use. Of these the former was always stressed
in OE., the latter occasionally. In ME., however, the original
meaning of *mis-* is often weakened, which, hence, partly loses
the accent" (Morsbach § 40). In Mod. E. the verb has the
accent, or level stress takes place (Sweet).

a) in the *Troy-Book*:

mýsdon, 5088.
mýs lyket, 1698.
mýsschap, mýsshapon, 5482, 7751, 7758.

b) in the *Morte Arthure*:

mísdoo, 126.
mýshappene, mýshappenede, 3454, 3767.
mýskaries, mýskaryede, 1237, 2872; but
myscáryede, 1778.
myse-bíde, 3083.

c) in *Piers the Plowman*:

misbeliĉue, mýsbileue, A 11, 71; B 15, 402.
mísdoth, mis-dude, mýsdo, mýsdon, A 3, 118; A 4, 86; B 15, 107,
    252; B 16, 212; B 18, 339; but
mysdó, B 18, 97.
mýs-hap, mýshappe, mýshappes, B 3, 327; A 8, 79; C 12, 187; but
myshápped, B 10, 283.
mýs-reuleth, B 9, 59.
mýsseide, B 16, 127; but
mis-séid, myssáyde, A 5, 51; C 21, 353.
mýsshape, B 7, 95.

mýs-wonne, B 13, 42; but also
mis-béode, A 7, 45.
myslíked, C 17, 311.
myspénde, C 11, 185.

8. Denominatives have the accent of the Noun from which they are derived.

a) in the *Troy-Book*:

wélcomd, wélcomed, wélcomth, wélcomyt, 513, 1793, 3430, 5406, 7912, 13342.

When we find in Browning (*Sordello,* p. 61) the verse:
Welcomed him at Roncaglia! Sadness now
we must look upon this as an example of stress-shifting („Takt-umstellung“).

b) in *Piers the Plowman*:

wél-comen, A 6, 114; B 18, 174; but also
welcóme, welcómeth, B 15, 21; B 20, 59.

Chapter II.

B. The Romance Element.

The differences between ME. and Mod. E. in the accentuation of words of Romance derivation are much more numerous than in those of Germanic origin. The question as to whether this greater difference in accentuation in the alliterative poems of the fourteenth century points to a real divergence in the spoken language, as compared with our present practice, has not been settled until now. Luick (*Anglia* XI, p. 394 sq.) pronounces the following opinion on this point: "Of course the alliteration affects the beginning of the accented syllables. Romance words alliterate with the same Germanic stress as in Mod. E., and we have no occasion for doubting that this accentuation prevailed in the fourteenth century. It is true, we occasionally find that prefixes of Romance words bear the alliteration, which in Mod. E. are unstressed... It is difficult to assume that these prefixes were really accented; we must look upon such cases as offences against the metre, such as may occasionally occur in the best poets... It is difficult to assign a reason for this irregularity which is all the more striking, when we consider the general regularity of the metre (in the *Troy-Book*)... In certain cases, indeed, it seems to me not impossible that the accentuation differed from that in Mod. E."

These remarks hardly bring us nearer to a solution of problem that presents itself in the difference of accentuation in Romance words in ME. as compared with Mod. E. "In certain cases" Luick accepts such a difference, but declares that the cause of it is difficult to explain, and is inclined to see "offences against metre" ("metrische Verstösse") in the "occasional" accentuation of the prefixes. Now, however, cases of such accentuation do not occur merely "occassionally", but are, on the contrary, fairly numerous in our texts, and it is hardly satisfactory to reduce them to errors in metre. Where the existence of these differences is insured by the metre, and when they show themselves not merely in one, but in all of our texts, as well as in others, we are forced to assume, either that such accentuations represented the actual pronunciation of the poets, or that their alliteration was a mere empty device, existing only for the eye. The latter assumption is surely hardly probable.

In the following arrangement of our material, we class the examples as *Substantives, Adjectives* (including *Adverbs*), and *Verbs,* and separate dissyllables from polysyllables, words with prefixes, from those without them, words with abnormal, from those with modern stress, and finally obsolete expressions from those still in use.

I. Substantives.

1. Dissyllabic Nouns (including trisyllables with final unaccented e) with Prefixes and present accentuation.

a) in the *Troy-Book*:

cómford, cómfordes, 213, 3595, 5806, 5900.
cómpas, cúmpas, 523, 2710, 3032, 5604.
prélates, 206.
présens, 250, 1896, 1963, 4152, 7936.
prólogé, 96, 2207.
rélikes, 11391.
súbiectes, 3545.

These have the English stress, viz. on the first syllable, because the prefix was no longer felt as such, and the words no longer had the value of compounds.
míschefe, mýschefe, 6493, 9055, 11556.

The French particle *mes-* corresponded to the English *mis*, and was treated like the latter. In the *Man. Vocab.* we have *míschiefe,* 53, 12. In English words with *mis-* the stress varied (cf. pp. 8, 19), and so also here. We find, therefore, also *mys-cháunce,* 3509, but in the *Man. Voc.*: a *míschance,* 21, 42; and also (*to*) *mischánce,* 22, 20.

Words with other prefixes:

assént, 2131, 3221, 3575, 3666, 5189, 8942, 9803.

defáute, 9376.

defénce, defénse, deffénce, 1740, 2128, 4715, 5239, 6423, 9518, 9563.

degré, 13436.

delítes, 4417.

dispít, dispíte, 7945, 10684.

enténte, intént, 27, 575, 2503, 2709, 2916, 3109, 3139, 3677, 11364.

escháunge, 7904.

offénce, 9700.

redrésse, 2221, 3603.

reprófe, 2034.

usually do not draw back the accent on the particle. A sure proof of this is found in the occurrence of many such words with apheresis, (cf. Behrens, *Franz. Lehnwörter im ME.* 1886, p. 64), e. g. *defence* and *fense; dispense* and *spense,* &c. But in the *Troy-Book* we find some of those words with stress on the prefix:

défense, 2692:

> *What defense has þou done to our dere goddes?*

where we might, however, assume the absence of the first rime-letter. Levins has only *defénce,* 63, 24.

délites, délitis, 3346, 3350, 3560.

The accentuation of such words varied, therefore, as it does also in Shakspere (König, p. 72), in *dísease* and *diséase; dístinct* and *distínct; éxcuse* and *excúse; révenge* and *revénge; récord* and *recórd.* In the last of these words the stress varied until within recent times (cf. Flügel's Dict. s. v.). The *Man. Voc.* has only *a récorde,* 171, 18.

We find also a varying accent in:

compláint, 1516, 3514; and *cómplaint,* 3280, 3293, 10767. In Chaucer, *Compl. of Mars,* the word occurs three times with the stress on the prefix, but the verb is accented on the second syllable.

Nouns with parasitic *c* before *s* + consonant, according to ten Brink, do not allow a removal of the stress to the first syllable (cf. ten Brink, § 285). In our text:

astáte (where *a* = *c*), 21, 251, 365, 1865; but also
ástate, 3251, 3311, 4809, 12450, where, in each case, the first
    syllable is the bearer of the chief-letter.

b) in the *Morte Arthure*:

Of words already mentioned above we find here:
defáwtes, 2928.
degré, 84; (*Man. Voc.*: a *degrée*, 46, 36).
disspíte, 3163.
mýschefe, 667.
relíkkes, 4207.
asáwtte, assáwtte, 1697, 3012, 3053.

With a prefix the force of which was no longer recognised as such:
ábsens, absénce, 1596, 3447.
cóndethe, cóndethes, cóundyte, cúñdit, 201, 444, 475, 3148, 3483
cóunge, 479.
cóntek, cónteke, 2721, 3069, 4177.
prófyre, 1257.
ráunsone, 1528.
rémenaunt, 1553 (in ME. still trisyllabic).
réscowe, réscows, 433, 1953, 3859, 4137.
súbarbe, súbbarbes, 2466, 4043.
súrcott, súrcotte, 2434, 3252.

Also:
cóncelle, cónsayle, cóunsaile, 144, 243, 259, 291, 1023, 1959, 2395.

With the same stress in Chaucer and in Mod. E. but in Minot still with French accentuation:

> At Pariss toke þai þaire counsaile
> Whilk pointes might þam most availe (III, 45).

c) in *Piers the Plowman*:

cónseille, cóunseil, A 2, 108; B 19, 75, 312.
méschaunce, C 4, 97; B 14, 75, differs from the present accentuation, but cf. p. 58 above.

áccesse, A 5, 210 (cf. Oxf. Dict. and Dial. Dict. s. v.). This accentuation, agreeing with the modern one, may be accepted for this passage:

And after al this surfet· an accesse he hadde.

for which we find in B with the missing rime-letter supplied:

And after al this excesse· he had an accidie.

In Chaucer we have *accésse:*

The which can helen thee of thyn accesse (Troil. II, 1315).

íssue, C 19, 221.

présent, B 19, 304.

súrfet, A 7, 252.

tréspas, A 1, 95.

To these the remarks on p. 58 apply.

récorde, C 4, 346. Cf. remark on p. 58.

The following examples leave the prefix unstressed (cf. p. 58):

afféres, C 7, 152.

alárme, B 20, 91.

apéel, a-péles, C 3, 186, 244; C 20, 284.

assáy, B 10, 253.

defáute, defáutes, A 2, 109; A 5, 6.

In the A-text 7, 113 we find apparently the accentuation *défaute:*

And thauh ʒe dyen for de-faute· the deuel haue that reeche!

But as in B and C *defaute* has been replaced by *dole, deul,* we should perhaps not assume the accentuation *défaute.*

delýtes, A 2, 68.

dispít, C 9, 184.

d) in *Richard the Redeles:*

Here we have only to record words already discussed:

entént, enténte, Pr. 79; 2, 99.

estáte, Pr. 82.

In the words of the preceding section we have merely to point to the agreement in the accentuation with that of the present day.

2. Dissyllabic Nouns (including trisyllables with final unaccented e) with Prefixes and with Accentuation differing from the present one.

a) in the *Troy-Book*:

díssait, díssayt, díssayet, dýssait, 254, 1185, 3801, 4291, 4436, 4459, 10239, 12656. (Verb, below). In Middleton (Schulz, p. 24), but at the beginning of the verse:

What deceit means 'tis English yet to him (V, 33).

déuyse, 6079:

> *By deuyse of the duke, þat doghtie was aye.*

In Chaucer always with stress on the second syllable. Cf. the verb, below.

dísseese, dýsese, 3326, 5021.

In Shakspere (König pp. 72, 74):

Thou disease of a friend. and not himselfi (Tim. III, 1, 56).

In Middleton (Schulz, p. 24):

Whose disease once I undertook to cure (IV, 339).

In Chaucer always *diséase.*

díssire, díssyre, désyre, 558, 2426, 4896, 4920, 7421, 11845, 11865, 13138.

púrsuet, 4853, 8882:

Syn I with prayer, ne with pursuet, preset not þeraftur.

. The same accentuation occurs also in Chaucer (*Troil.* II, 959):

> *But lack of pursuit make it in thy slouthe.*

and probably also in:

> *In titering, and pursuite, and delayes* (ib. 1744).

In Shakspere (Abbot, p. 396) the word stands near the beginning of the verse:

In pursuit of the thing she would have stay (Sonn 143).

So also in Marlowe:

> *In pursuit of the city's overthrow* (I, 50).

réward, 1879, 2405, 4543:

Probably neither the prefix was here felt as such, nor was the French origin of the word recognised, which was therefore stressed like an English one.

abséns, 2954:

> *In absens of þi souerayne, for saghes of pepull.*

Here perhaps the first rime-letter is wanting.

b) in the *Morte Arthure*:

rénoune, 1732:

> *Thynke one riche renounc of the Rounde Table.*

In Chaucer the stress of this word varies (ten Brink § 285)
subárbes, 3122:

> *Boyes in the subarbes bourdene ffulle heghe.*

With the same stress in Chaucer:

In the suburbes of a toun, quod he (Can. Yeom. Prol. 104).

c) in *Piers the Plowman*:

déceyte, B 18, 331:

> *For the dede that thei dede· thi deceyte it made.*

The same alliteration also in the C-text. Cf. above p. 61.
désert, C 4, 293:

> *A desert for som doynge· derne other elles.*

dýspayre, B 20, 163:

> *And threwe drede of dyspayre· a dozein myle aboute.*

Similarly in C. With this accentuation the word is found
only here.

réles, A 7, 83:

> *To ha reles and remission· on that rental I be-leeue.*

Also in B and C.

répast, C 10, 148:

Whar he may rathest haue a repast· other a rounde of bacon.

For the accentuation:

rénon, B Pr. 158.

réward, réwarde, C 5, 40; B 17, 265. Cf. above pp. 61, 62.

assétz, B 17, 237, was perhaps still looked upon as French and
hence preserved its original stress.

French accentuation is also seen in:

enquéstes, C 14, 85.

prophétes, B 19, 141.

the latter also with this stress in the *Pearl,* 831, but *próphetes*
in *Cleanness,* 1300.

d) in *Richard the Redeles*:

déuyse, 3, 178:

> And iche day a newe deuyse· it dullith my wittis.

répreff, Pr. 56:

> ffor reson is no repreff· be the rode of Chester!

In the *Troy-Book*, *reprófe* cf. p. 58. Also in Chaucer with stress on the second syllable.

résceyte, 2, 98:

> And reson hath rehersid· the resceyte of all.

In Chaucer the stress varies: in *Ch. Yem.* 800 *réceit*; ib. 813 *recéit*.

When we find in Shakspere, &c. apparent accentuations like *déceit, dísease*, we should not attach too much importance to such cases. Similar apparent accentuations (most of them again at the beginning of the verse) occur also in poets of our own time. So for example in

Browning (*Parleyings*):

Surface once all a-work! "Ay, such a Suite." (p. 226).

Discords and resolutions turn aghast (p. 233).

In Arnold (*Balder*):   ...and hold

Converse; his speech remains, though he be dead (p. 119).

     ...is my enforced

Absence from fields where I could nothing aid (p. 136).

(*Merope*):   ...and for him

Exile abroad more safe than heirship here (p. 362).

The stress in *exile* varies partly till the present day, because noun and verb have mutually influenced each other. Cf. Flügel's Dict., but also the Oxf. Dict. s. v.

In Boyer's Dictionary occur the following accentuations that come under this division and that derserve notice:

accéss (in Levins *áccesse*), *áquests*, *commént*, *concépt*, *concért*, *cónsult* (now obsolete as subst.), *contrást*, *invóice*, *perfúme* (cf. Encycl. Dict.), *porténet*, *prétence*, *provóst*, *recórd*.

In Bailey: *ássent*, *concréte* (subst. and adj.), *contóur* (cf. Oxf.-Dict.), *contrást*, *dévice* (and *devíse*), *discóunt*, *engíne* (cf. Oxf.-Dict.), *exíle*, *ingréss*, *invóice*, *perfúme* (cf. Encycl. Dict.), *precínct*, *preságe*, *prodúce*, *recórd*, *réssort*, *survéy*.

Bei Levins: *contráct*, *desért*.

3. Dissyllabic Nouns (including trisyllables with final unaccented *e*) without Prefix and present Accentuation.

In these words the French stress has throughout been replaced by the English one, i. e. the first syllable is accented.

a) in the *Troy-Book*:

déuer, 234, 590, 764.
tóurment, 3295.
ázure, ázoure, 193, 765, 3355,

b) in the *Morte Arthure*:

córage, 536, 1725, 1922.
méruail, méruayle, 2682, 2905.
rébawde, rébawdez, 1333, 1416, 1705.
sólace, sólauce, 54, 153, 239, 354, 659.
véscounte, véscownte, vícounte, víscounte, výscownte, 1984, 2024, 2047, 2050, 3167.

c) in *Piers the Plowman*:

déuer, déuoir, déuor, déuore, B 11, 277; B 13. 212; B 14, 136, 150, 153; C 18, 92.
érmite, érmytes, éremites, A Pr. 50; C 1, 3, 30; C 9, 183.
óffices, B 15, 379.

4. Dissyllabic Nouns (including trisyllables with final unaccented *e*) without Prefix and with Accentuation differing from the present one.

a) in the *Morte Arthure*:

rómance, 3440.
In Chaucer the stress varies: *Book of the Duch.* 48 *rómaunce; Troil.* III, 980 *romáunce.* In the *Rom. of Part.* 6417 we have *rómans*:

What me shall call thys romans souerain.

In Minot VII, 169 perhaps also *rómance.* This accentuation is still heard at the present day in vulgar speech.

b) in *Piers the Plowman*:

vságe, B 7, 87:

Late vsage be ʒoure solace· of seyntes lyues redynge.

This French accentuation is also found in Chaucer, *Prol.* 110; *Prioresse,* 54, 75; but *úsage, Leg. of Phil.* 110.

Boyer has the following examples in which the accentuation differs from the present one:

cámpain, cément (noun and verb), *crávat, mánure* (so also Encycl. Dict.), *placárd, trefóil, triphthóng* (but *diphthong*).

In Bailey: *bázar, cadénce, chémise, devóir, dívan, fermént, mirró(u)r, prismóid, rómance, sapphíre,* (*spheróid*), *turmóil.*

In Levins: *legáte, parént, cément.*

5. Nouns of three or more Syllables with Prefix and modern stress.

In Chaucer's accentuation of such words we find a tendency to draw back the stress by two syllables, so that the chief and the secondary accents change places (cf. ten Brink, § 286).

a) in the *Troy-Book*:

cómpany, cúmpany, 325, 2939, 4023, 4074, 4078, 4161, 4228, 4566, 4617, 4886, 5404, 5486, 6158, 6210, 6217, 6332, 6488, 6848, 7222, 7844, 8159, 8941, 9046.

cónseruatours, 8779, which still has this stress.

cóuenant, cóuenaund, cóuenaunt, cóuenaundes, 643, 705, 712, 999.

déstyne, déstyny, 583, 2522.

compássion, 11985.

émperour(e), 314, 3670.

The accentuation of:

assémblis, assémbly, assémely, 57, 2929, 5897, 6299, 6637.

atténdant, 3369.

encháuntment, encháuntementes, 163, 773, 947 is that of the corresponding verbs.

aváuntage, 7045:

In Chaucer the stress of this word varies:

Frankel's Tale 44: *avántage,* of three syllables; *Man of L.* 631: *ávantàge,* of four syllables.

expéryment, 13217.
indítyng (verbal noun), 5423.

b) in the *Morte Arthure*:

Shifting of accent also in:
assémble, 1578.
déstanye, désteny, 1563, 3436, 3779.
émperour, 286,- 414, 507, 1326, 1660, 1673, 2244, 2255 (cf. ten Brink § 286).
óccidente, 2360.
rétenuz, rétenewys, 1334, 1665, 2664, 3572.

With apheresis:
skómfitoure, skómfyture, and also *skómfite,* 1561, 1644, 2335; the accentuation of the verb below. The *Man. Voc.* has *discomféyture.*

So also:
despýsere, 538.
discóuerours, skóuerours, 3117, 3118.

c) in *Piers the Plowman*:

With stress drawn back, as above:
appúrtenaunce, B 15, 184.
cómissarie, cómmissarie, A 2, 154; A 3, 138; B 15. 234.
cómpaignye, cómpanye, B 13, 160; C 17, 341.
cónsistorie, cónstorie, B Pr. 99; A 3, 32, 137; B 3, 318; B 15, 234.

The same stress at present, or with accent on the second syllable.
cóntenaunce, cóntinaunce, cóntinence, cóntynaunce, cóntynence, cúntinaunce, A Pr. 24; B 5, 183; C 12, 164, 177; B 13, 111; C 19, 73.
cónysaunce, C 19, 188.
cóuenant, cóuenaunt, cóuenaunte, A 5, 184; A 7, 30; B 14, 151; C 15, 216.
déstenye, A 7, 261.
émperesse, émperour, B 13, 165.
éuydences, C 9, 263.
expérimentz, B 10, 212.
excécutours, exécutores, exécutours, C 3, 189; B 5, 266; B 20, 288.
résidue, A 5, 240; A 7, 93.

In *prócuratour*, B 19, 253, the stress has been removed from the fourth to the first syllable. Cf. the form *prócutòur* in Chaucer, *Freres T.* 298, and the Mod. E. *próctor*. Cf. also the accentuation of the verb *prócure* below.

acórdaunce, C 4, 339.

allówaunce, a-lóuance, alówaunce, C 10, 271; B 11, 215; B 14, 109; C 16, 290.

assémble, B Pr. 217.

conterróller, C 12, 298

have the stress of their respective verbs.

In *affíaunce*, B 16, 238, the prefix was unstressed (cf. ten Brink, § 285), as it is at present. Chaucer, *Shipm. Tale* 139, has the French accentuation *affiánce*.

The same applies also to:

apárail, appárail, C 7, 30; A 9, 111.

arérage, arrérage, C 10, 274; B 11, 124. (Cf. Oxf. Dict. s. v.).

esschéker, A 4, 26.

supprióure, B 5, 171, has the same stress as *prióur*.

6. Nouns of three or more Syllables with Prefix and with Accentuation differing from the present one.

a) in the *Troy-Book*:

áunter, áuntres, 67, 3883, 6725.

Only the dissyllabic form occurs here as bearer of the alliteration. The fuller form *áventure* had undoubtedly the same stress. It is found frequently in our texts as well as in other ME. works. The syncope *áunter* proves this accentuation.

cómaundement, cómmaundement, 438, 491, 511, 1714, 2163, 2899, 3316, 4442, 10280, 10517, 11591, 13882.

Of this accentuation also there are numerous examples in our texts. Both noun and verb have the stress on the first syllable, and this accentuation must really have obtained, as is proved by the Northern forms *cómmanent* &c. (cf. Behrens, *Franz. Lehnwörter*, p. 66). It is also found in Minot:

> *Schípmen sóne war éfter sént*
> *To hére þe kínges cúmandmént* (III, 50).

So also the verb:

He cúmand þán þat mén suld fáre (III, 53).

cóndiscoun, 9229.

In the *Man. Voc.* we also find *cóndition,* where it is quoted as verb.

cónfusion, 2319, with the same stress as the verb *cónfound* below. Chaucer also accentuates *cónfus: Troil.* IV, 356; *Sec. Non. T.* 463; *Knight T.* 1372.

cóniuracioun, 13216. Cf. the verb *conjurate* in the Oxf. Dict.

córupcioun, 10787. Cf. *corrupt* in the Oxf. Dict. where the remark is made: "By Chaucer and Gower often stressed on first syllable." In this and similar words the prefix was no longer felt as such, and the stress drawn back on the first syllable. So also in the following:

déleberacion, 2457.

délyuerans, 2897, so also the verb below.

déuocioun, 4470, 4551. Cf. the accentuation *dévout* in Spenser (Günther p. 21):

Yet of the devout people is adored (530 b).

discrecioun, discresion, 9237, 11261. For the accentuation *díscreet* cf. ten Brink § 285, and the verse of Webster (Meiners p. 17):

Lies in his wardrobe: he's a discreet fellow (*WD.* 14 a).

díshonesty, dýshoner, dýshonour, 528, 1005, 1852, 3643, 4199, 5038. Cf. Chaucer:

If of hir body dishonest she be (*Maunc. T.* 110)

pérsiueraunce, 2655. In Chaucer with stress on the second syllable both in noun and verb. So also in Shakspere (cf. Schipper II, 156).

présumpcoun, 5114.

púrviaunce, 1043. In Minot:

I prais no thing his puruiaunce (VII, 146).

In Shakspere (König p. 74; Abbot p. 396): *púrveyor* (*M.* I, 6, 22).

répentaunse, 4885. In Chaucer:

To hem that been in repentaunce and drede (*Kn. T.* 918).

He wiste that a man was repentaunt (*Prol.* 228).

In Wyatt (Schipper II, 158) *répentance*. Cf. also the accentuation of the verb in the *Morte Arthure* below.

súccessoures, súccessours, 4198, 4455. Cf. Schipper II, 160.

In Dryden (*Secret Love* V, 1):

> *I here declare you rightful successor.*

The accentuation *súccess* is not unknown in Modern E., especially in the North. In Scotland I have often heard it, even from clergymen and teachers. It belongs however to vulgar speech (cf. Storm, *Engl. Phil.* I², 813).

b) in the *Morte Arthure*:

áuenture, áuntire, áwntere, áwntire, 642, 1905, 2244, 2617.

cómmandement, cómmandment, cómmandmente, cómmaundement, 131, 581, 739, 1514, 4150.

cóndycyone, 1511.

púrueaunce, 688.

For these words cf. the remarks on pp. 67, 68.

cónfessour, 4314. For this accentuation cf. the Oxf. Dict. s. v. Especially in the phrase "E(a)dward the Confessor" this accentuation is still heard (cf. Cent. Dict. s. v.). Also in Shakspere (König, p. 75, Abbot, p. 394) the first syllable is often stressed: *H*⁸ I, 1, 218; *H*⁸ I, 2, 149; *R. J.* II, 6, 21; *R. J.* III, 3, 49; *M. M.* IV, 3, 133. So also in Middleton (Schulz, p. 30). Levins, *Man. Voc.*, accentuates: *conféssour*.

prócessione, 4014.

prótteccione, 2410. For these words cf. the remarks on *córupcioun,* p. 68, and the accentuation *prótector* in Shakspere (König, p. 75), *H*⁶ III, 1, 112.

injúryc, 663, which is of four syllables here, has the stress of the modern *injúrious*.

c) in *Piers the Plowman*:

áuenture, áunter, B 3, 72; C 9, 40.

cómaundement, cómmaundemens, cómaundour, A 3, 280; C 4, 413; C 12, 143.

cónfessour, cónfession, cónfessioun, A 3, 36; A 4, 132; C 6, 195; A 10, 131; B 11, 70; C 11, 53; A 12, 41; B 12, 176; C 13, 196; B 14, 186; B 19, 345; B 20, 212, 326, 369.

córupcioun, B 20, 98.

présumpcioun, présumpciun, A 11, 42; B 11, 413. So also the
verb below.

répentance, répentaunce, A 5, 43, 103; B 5, 182; C 7, 12; C 11, 214;
B 17, 298, 301.

For the accentuation of these words cf. the remarks on
p. 67 sq.

cónstellacion, A 10, 142. Cf. the modern verb *constellate*, in
which the stress still varies (Oxf. Dict. s. v.).

cóntemplacion, C 8, 305; C 19, 73. Here also the stress varies
in the verb.

désperacion, B 17, 307. So also in Chaucer, *ABC* 21. Cf. the
modern *désperate*.

pérmutacion, A 3, 243. So also the verb *pérmute* below.

pérsecucion, C 13, 205. Cf. the modern verb *pérsecute*.

réstitucioun, B 5, 232; B 17, 235, 313.

rémembraunce, C 6, 11.

cóncepcion, cóncepcioun, A 10, 178; B 11, 328. So also the
verb, below.

cóntricion, cóntricioun, B 11, 81, 130; C 11, 53; B 12, 176; B 14,
16, 82, 87; B 19, 328, 342, 344; B 20, 212, like the modern
adj. *cóntrite*.

prófession, A 1, 98. So also the verb below.

rélacion, C 4, 344, 346, 363.

réligion, réligioun, réligiun, C 4, 203; A 5, 37; B 6, 153; C 6, 151;
A 8, 35; A 9, 82; B 10, 76; A 11, 199, 202, 206, 208; B 13, 286;
B 15, 85.

rémission, A 7, 83; A 11, 277.

súggestion, B 7, 69.

The same accentuation also in Levins, *Man. Voc.*, but the
verb with stress on the second syllable.

súspecion, C 18, 315.

absólucion, A 8, 67, as still the verb *absólve*.

For the accentuation of the following words see the remarks on p. 68 under *córupcioun*.

córectoures, B 10, 284.

éxperimentis, A 11, 157.

índulgences, B 17, 253.

óbedyence, B 12, 38.

próuisours, A 2, 148; A 3, 142; A 4, 116.

For the accentuation *innócence,* B 17, 286 cf. the adject. below, p. 80.

sustinaunce, C 23, 7:

That thou toke to lyue by· to sustinaunce and clothes.

In the B-text:

That thow toke to thi bylyf· to clothes and to sustenaunce.

From the defective alliteration no conclusion can be drawn as to the stress of this word.

d) in *Richard the Redeles:*

díscrecioun, 2, 110. Cf. p. 68.

It may perhaps be assumed that most of the words quoted above under 6., as examples in which the stress differs from the modern accentuation, really had the stress indicated by the alliteration, or at least that the accentuation varied. A direct proof for such deviations from modern usage we find in some similar examples from Levins. So he accentuates:

óbseruance, 21, 46.

perséuerance, 22, 2.

euídence, 63, 44.

préferment, 68, 7.

ádolescence, 96, 26.

prósperitie, 110, 25.

épistil, 128, 28.

discomféyture, 191, 20.

dishonóure, 222, 47.

In Boyer also: *adulátor, circúmstance, compétency, compromise, condémnation, condénsation, cónfessor, conflágration, cónservation, cónventicle* (cf. Oxf. Dict.), *co-óperation, décampment, decorátor, dedicátor, demónstration, diápason, disàdvantage, immórtality, inválid, páramour, parathésis, procúracy, promóntory, prosecútor, reláxation, reprobàte, revénu, retínue.*

In Bailey the following examples: *acatalépsy, adólescence, anabásis, ancéstry, anécdote, apogée, appánage, assistánce, comprómise* (subst. and verb), *conséquence (in Astrology), conservátor, consuetúde, continuátor, cónventicle, denominátor, diátribe, dísaster, ecphásis, elevátor, emígrant, émpirick, emulátor, epexégesis, exégesis, explicátor, explorátor, exterminátor, extirpátor, hypocrite, imbécility, immórtality, impétus, inápplication, íncensory, angle of incídence, indústry (?), innovátor, insígnificancy, instigátor, interpolátor, inválid, metempsýchosis, ópponent, precédent, procurátor, prógnosis, prolocútor, provóstry, recúsants, renegáde, repértory, resolvénd, retícence, retínue, revénue, supplíant, sýllepsis.*

7. Nouns of three and more Syllables without Prefix and modern Stress.

a) in the *Troy-Book*:

fántasi, fántasy, 2669, 9575.
fféueryere, 4040 (= February).
órdinaunce, 6189, 7136, 7367, 8829
sácramen, 3362.
tábernacle, 1671.
ýmagry, 1562, 1646.

b) in the *Morte Arthure*:

áncestres, áuncestres, áwncestrye, 276, 521, 1310, 1907.
áuditoure, 1673.
cónstable, 1585 (frequently in Chaucer, *M. of L.* 429, 437, 457, 469, 477).
díamawndis, 3297.
gárnisone, gárnysone, gárysone, 2471, 2655, 3007, 3105.
márynerse, 3652.
pótestate, 2327.
sépulture, 4340.

c) in *Piers the Plowman*:

áudience, áuditour, C 8, 94; B 19, 458.
bénefices, bénefys, bénfes, B 3, 312; C 4, 33; A 6, 101; A 11, 192.
béneson, B 13, 235.
cónstable, C 4, 256.
élementes, élementz, C 2, 17; B 18, 235.
équite, B 17, 304; B 19, 305.

órisouns, C 19, 160.
* únite,* C 4, 338; C 6, 10, 190; B 19, 325.
úsurer, C 7, 307.
euángelist, euángelye, B 11, 184; C 13, 101.
satisfáccion, C 17, 27.

d) in *Richard the Redeles*:
máyntenaunce, 3, 312.

8. Nouns of three and more Syllables without Prefix and with Accentuation differing from the present one.

a) in the *Troy-Book*:
ábilite, 4012.

The forms *ablete, abiltee,* current in the 14th till 16th cent. (Cf. Oxf. Dict.), in connection with *able,* explain this accentuation.
ástronamy, ástronomy, 742, 3999, 10635. So also in *P. P.*
dévinours, déuynours, 10634, 13836.

For *lámentacion, lámentacioun, lamentacoun,* 3294, 7156, 8035 cf. Luick, *Anglia* XI, 395.
sátisfaccioun, 5017 (cf. also 7, c), and the accentuation *sátisfactóry* in the *Man. Voc.* 107, 10.
fílosofers, phílosofer, phýlosofer, 400, 2624, 2637. Cf. Chaucer *Prol.* 295; *Frank T.* 833.
ljuyatan, 4446.
nóbilte, 1842, 1965, 7578, direct derivation from *noble,* like *ablete* from *able.*
páuilyon, páuylions, pávilions, 6024, 7755, 10744. So also in •*P. P.* and in Minot, IV, 63; XI, 32. In Levins: *pauíllion,* 165, 30.
sólemnite, sólempnite, sólenite, 2869, 2884, 3451, 3462, 3871, 7160, 10786. So also in *P. P.* and frequently the trisyllabic adj. *sólempne,* p. 79.

b) in the *Morte Arthure*:
léuetenaunte, 646.
páuyllyons, pávelyouns, 2478, 2624.
phílosophre, phýlosophers, phýlozophirs, 807, 3226, 3394, cf. above p. 73.

póssessione, 2608, cf. the accentuation of the verb *póssess,* Schipper II, 152.

maríners, 633, but cf. the accentuation above p. 72.

sólempnitec, 514.

c) in *Piers the Plowman:*

ástronomye, also the forms *ástronomycnes, ástrymyanes* (for *astronomers*), A 11, 152; B 15, 352; B 19, 236.

liéutenant, B 16, 47.

páueylon, páuilon, A 2, 43; C 4, 452.

póssessions, póssessioun, A 11, 197; B 11, 264, 267; B 12, 248; B 13, 301; B 14, 270; B 15, 525.

philosofye, B 15, 377, like *phílosopher.*

sátisfaccioun, B 14, 21, 94; B 17, 314. For these cf. above p. 73.

arbýtours, C 7, 382. With this accentuation we find the word in our texts only in this passage. It is probably a case of faulty alliteration.

cúratour, cúratoures, A 1, 169; B 10, 409; B 13, 13; B 15, 132; C 18, 292; B 19, 448.

For this word with its still varying stress cf. Oxf. Dict. s. v. Further examples with accent drawn back are the following:

dámpnacioun, B 12, 89.

diuinite, diuinour, díuynours, díuynour, A 11, 293; B 15, 373; C 16, 85, 123. So also the adj. p. 78 below.

félicite, B 20, 239.

fráternite, A 8, 179; B 11, 55; B 20, 365.

fýsician, phísiciene, C 19, 141; B 20, 313. In the *Man. Voc.* with present stress.

géneracioun, B 16, 220.

grámarienes, B 13, 72. Cf. *grámmar.*

méyntenour, C 4, 288, like *máyntenaunce,* p. 73.

sáluacion, sáuacion, sáuacioun, A 11, 274; B 11, 142; B 15, 490; C 18, 119. The same accentuation also in the *Man. Voc.* 157, 46.

mítigacion, mýtigacion, A 5, 252; C 7, 324.

téologye, théologie, théologye, A 2, 83; B 10, 374; A 11, 136; A 12, 9.

vírginite, vírgynyte, B 16, 203; C 19, 89.

ýpocrisye, B 20, 298.

d) in *Richard the Redeles*:

méyntenourz, 3, 268. See p. 74.

túrmentours, 3, 118. The same accentuation in Chaucer, *Fortune* 18; *Man of Lawe* 720; *Sec. Nonne* 527; and also in *Cleanness* 154. Cf. the verb, with the same accentuation, below.

In Boyer we find:

altérnation, arbitrátor-trix, architécture, balcòny, bénediction, bénefaction, bénefactor, calumniátor, cárnality, cósmeticks, gòndoleer, légatee, límpidity, lótophagi, máchination, multiplicánd, mythológist, oligárchy, operátor, opiniátiveness, overtúre, pantomìme, peculátor, quíntessence, sálamander, thermométer, (but *barómeter), tópographer* (but *typógrapher), tragédy* (but *cómedy), vindicátor.*

In Bailey:

ácademy (college &c. school or Seminary; in the Canting Dialect, a Brothel), ambáges, archíves, augúry, autópsy (cf. Oxf. Dict.), *balcóny, calentúre, cathéter, corridór, emulátor, equéry* (cf. Oxf. Dict.), *equipóise, feálty, fornicátor, harmónists, hýœna, hydróphobia, ignóminy, imitátor, libertíne, logomáchy, mágister, manía, marchíoness, marmóset, marquétry, marróquin, mediátor, memóirs, metallúrgist, metallúrgy, metéors, moderátor, operátor, pálissade, palíndrome, Philístines, polýhistor, pólygraphy, pólymathy, pontífice* (but Milton, *P. L.* X, 348 has *póntifice), presbýtery, probábilism, probábilists, royálness, satéllite, satýrist, sepúlchre, sepúlture, stimulátor, trapezóid, triángle, vindicátor.*

Accentuations like those quoted under 8: *lámentacioun, póssessione,* &c. we find also in the *Man. Voc.*:

sálatation, 165, 46.

embássage, 11, 39 (so also Boyer, and Bailey who gives this stress also to *embássy*).

anímall, 13, 44.

cáthedrall, 13, 47.

a *cardínall*, 14, 9.

díadéeme, 60, 19.

córiander, 80, 46.

nicrómancer, 81, 3.

villánie, 102, 28.

diétarie, 104, 1, (so also Bailey).

histórie, 104, 32 (like *story*).
bárbaritie, 109, 3.
feáltie, 109, 31, (so also Bailey).
húmiditie, 109, 41.
príncipalitie, 110, 17.

From such examples (when the stress is not placed wrongly, owing to a printer's error) we may probably conclude that also in the time of our alliterative poets the stress of many Romance words differed from the present one, and we should, therefore, not simply reject such abnormal accentuations.

9. Dissyllabic obsolete Nouns.

a) in the *Troy-Book*:

affráy, affrói, 4746, 7734. Cf. Oxf. Dict. s. v. and the verb below.
cómbranse, cómbraunse, cúmbranse, 2281, 9169, 12076, like the present *encumbrance.*

b) in the *Morte Arthure*:

affráye, 3226.
avówe, 206, 308, 347.
dyspéns, 538. So also in Chaucer, like the present *expense.*
orfráyes, 2142, Old French *orfrois* (Stratm.-Bradl. *ME. Dict.*).
Accented *órfrays* in the *Rom. of the Rose,* 562, 869, 1076.

c) in *Piers the Plowman*:

cómbraunce, cúmburance, A 2, 137; C 6, 191; C 13, 245; B 18,
· 263; C 19, 174.
mál-ese, C 9, 233.
méynprise, A 4, 75; but *meynpríse,* B 16, 264. Cf. the verb, below.
In the *Man. Voc.* 148, 2 *a mainprýse.*
spélonkes, B 14, 270. In modern Dutch and German with stress on second syllable.

d) in *Richard the Redeles*:

cómbraunce, 3, 113.
párceit, Pr. 17, like the verb *pérceyue,* p. 91 below.

10. Obsolete Nouns of three or more Syllables.

a) in the *Troy-Book*:

sólstacion, 10637.

b) in the *Morte Arthure*:

avánttwarde, aváwewarde, aváwwarde, 324, 2024, 2051, 3168, 3764, but
ávawmwarde, 2829.
aváwmbrace, 2568.
avéntaile, 910, 2572.   Cf. the verb *avent* below.

   In Chaucer, *Cl. T.* 1148: *àventáille;* cf. Oxf. Dict. s. v.
cóuytise, 11328, cf. the adj. p. 78 below.
avísement, 148, cf. Oxf. Dict. *advisement.*
enbúschement, 1407.
encórownmentes, 4197.
fórreours, 2450, 2901, 3017.
spýcerye, 162.   Also in Chaucer, *Sir Thop.* 142.
sekádrisses, 2283.

c) in *Piers the Plowman*:

áccidie, B 5, 366.   In Gower, *Confí* II, 19, stressed on the second
   syllable.   Cf. Oxf. Dict. s. v.
álconomye, A 11, 157.   In Gower, *Conf.* II, 48, stressed on the
   second syllable.   Cf. Oxf. Dict. *alchemy.*
álmaries, C 17, 88, cf. *ambry* in the Oxf. Dict.
ámpolles, A 6, 11, cf. *ampul* in the Oxf. Dict.
asísours, C 23, 290, cf. *sizar* with apheresis.
cóueitise, cóueityse, cóuetise, cóuetyse, cóuetyze, A Pr. 58; B 2, 85;
   C 7, 39; A 11, 18; B 13, 391; C 13, 241; B 14, 238.   So also
   Rom. of the Rose, 203; cf. Oxf. Dict. s. v.
ensámple, ensámples, ensáumple, A 1, 146; C 2, 195; A 4, 119;
   A 5, 17; B 10, 294, 468; C 11, 243; C 14, 201.
espírit, C 15, 27, cf. ten Brink § 285.
fénestres, B 15, 199; B 18, 15.   In *Arthour and Merlin,* 815
   accented on the second syllable.
fóreioures, B 20, 80.
nóunpowere, B 17, 310.

párinterlinarie, B 11, 298.
régrateres, régratour, régratye, A 3, 81; C 4, 82, 118; A 5, 140.
rétenaunce, A 2, 35.

d) in *Richard the Redeles*:
déseueraunce, A 2, 35.

II. Adjectives (and Adverbs).

1. The following adjectives and adverbs usually
conform in their accentuation to their corresponding
substantives, more rarely to their corresponding verbs.

a) in the *Troy-Book*:

áunterous, áuntrus, ántrus, 537, 2186, 3753, 4087, 6216, 6392,
6640, 6861, 7883 accented like *áunter,* pp. 67, 69.
cóntynually, 7419, so also the verb below.
cóucnable, 7951, like *cóuenant*; cf. Oxf. Dict. s. v.
cóuetous, cóuetus, 193, 259, 1808, 13820, like *cóuityse,* p. 77.
díscrete, 5523, like *díscrecioun,* p. 68.   Cf. also the varying stress
of *dístinct, distínct,* in Shakspere (König, p. 72).
dýssirus, déssyrous, díssyrus, 3799, 6155, 8003; cf. *díssire,* p. 61
and ten Brink § 287.
présumptius, 3847, like the noun, p. 68.
déuyne, 2542.   Cf. the accentuation in Shakspere (König, p. 73;
Schmidt, p. 1413); some of these at the beginning of the
verse:
The divine Desdemona. What is she (O. II, 1, 73).
Thou divine Imogen, what thou endurest (Cym. II, 1, 62).
Thou divine Nature, how thyselft thou blason'st (Cym. IV, 2, 170).

In Webster (Meiners, p. 16):
We cannot better please the divine power (W. D. 34 a).

In Middleton (Schulz, p. 25):
I find her circled in with divine writs (II, 367).
And kindling divine flames in fervent prayers (IV, 433).

In Jonson (Wilke, p. 40):
Of divine blessings would not serve a state (V. II, 198).
and six additional examples.   With Schipper, II, 152, we have

here probably to assume a „hovering stress" („schwebende Betonung").

sólempne, 1413, 2002, 2497, 2853, 2915, 2973, 2986, 3362, 4338, 4660, 5364, like the noun p. 74.

dispítiously, dispítously, dispítously, dispítus, 3889, 4744, 5099, 5111, 6494, 7652, 13173. For the subst. cf. p. 58 sq.

b) in the *Morte Arthure*:

áwntrouseste, 1624. For the noun p. 69 sq.

deuótly, devóttly, 296, 347, cf. *déuocioun*, p. 68; also ten Brink § 288.

rélygeous, 4334, like the subst. p. 70.

rénownde, rénownnd, 1994, 2372, 2912, like the subst. p. 62.

córageous, 338; examples of the same stress in Oxf. Dict. s. v.

méruailous, méruayllous, méruaylous, méruelyous, méruelyousteste, 129, 236, 260, 428, 2287. For the subst. cf. p. 64.

rébawdous, 456, like the subst., p. 64.

sólemply, sólempnely, sólempnylye, 525, 1948, 3196, 3805. For the subst. cf. p. 74.

c) in *Piers the Plowman*:

cómpanable, B 15, 213. So also Chaucer, *Shipm. T.* 4. Cf. Oxf. Dict. s. v.

cónfus, B 10, 136. In Chaucer the stress varies: *cónfus Kn. T.* 1372; *confús H. of F.* 427.

déuowtliche, C 18, 245. Cf. the subst. p. 68.

dílitáble, A 1, 32, like the verb below. Cf. also ten Brink § 287.

présent, A 2, 62.

présumptuously, A 11, 42, like the subst. pp. 68, 69.

rélatif, C 4, 357.

réligious, réligiouse, B 4, 120; C 6, 148, 165; B 12, 36; B 15, 302, 312, 335, 506, 512; B 20, 58. Cf. the subst. p. 70.

ófficiales, B 2, 173. In the *Rom. of the Rose* 6420, with stress on the second syllable.

innócent, innócentz, B 7, 41; A 8, 51. Cf. the subst. p. 71, but also ten Brink, § 287.

2. Adjectives (and Adverbs) which are not derived from Substantives or Verbs, or of which the corresponding Parts of Speech do not occur in our Texts.

a) in the *Troy-Book*:

áuenaunt, 7187. Cf. Oxf. Dict. s. v.

cóntrary, 4532, 4601, 11336. For the accentuation of this word cf. Oxf. Dict. s. v.; also Schipper II, 155, 307. Levins has modern stress.

próffitable, 3166.

éxcellent, 2433.

áusterne, 1976. For the form of this word cf. Oxf. Dict. s. v. and ib. the accentuation of the examples quoted.

cúrtesly, 829.

distráct, 3219. So also in Shakspere *J. C.* IV, 3, 155.

amírous, 3926:

> *Amirous vnto Maidens, & mony hym louyt.*

This accentuation is found only here. In the Oxf. Dict. too the examples from poets all have the stress on the first syllable. We should, therefore, perhaps assume the absence of the first rime-letter. The following verse from Browning, *Sordello* p. 253:

> *Amorous silence of the swooning-sphere,*

affords, of course, no proof for the accentuation *amórous*.

b) in the *Morte Arthure*:

ápparant, ápparaunt, 1944, 2606. The same accentuation *Rom. of the Rose*, 5. The subst. also occurs with this stress in Chaucer, *Squi. T.* 210, *Frank. T.* 412, 429, 874; *Hous of F.* 265.

áuenaunt, 2626, 3188, 3208, 3500.

dýuerse, 49, 1935. The second syllable is stressed in Chaucer, *Compl. unto P.* 17; *Book of the D.* 653; the first in *Frank. T.* 412. With the meaning "several", "sundry", the word is now written without final *e* and with first syllable stressed. When it signifies "different", it has the final *e* and the stress varies.

órrible, 1240.

prófitabille, 11.

récreaunt, 2334. So also *Rom. of the Rose*, 4090, but *Troil.* I, 814: *recréaunt*.

áusterene, áusteryne, 306, 414, 571, 670, 1326, 1510, 1623, 1906, 2256. Cf. p. 80 above.

géntileste, géntille, iéntille, jéntille, jéntylle, 115, 862, 904, 1161, 2088, 3411. So also in Chaucer.

sékerare, sékere, sékereste, sékerly, 439, 441, 478, 551, 593, 818, 831, 969, 1173, 1420, 1458, 1492, 1964, 2423, 3289, 3499, 4313.

This form is derived from the word *sicor*, known already in OE. (OHG. *sihhur*, MHG., Mod. HG. *sicher*, Dutch *zeker*), and not from *secure*, afterwards borrowed from the Romance. (Cf. also Morsbach § 115, Anm. 2). In early ME. these two forms, both derived from the Latin *securus*, have perhaps been con-founded. Cf. Kluge, *Etym. Wörterb.* s. v. In later poets we find *sécure* and *secúre*, now only *secúre*.

In Shaksp. (König, p. 73; Abbot, p. 396; Schmidt, p. 1415):
> *To lip a wanton in a secure couch* (*O.* IV, 1, 72).
> *Upon my secure hour thy uncle stole* (*H.* 1, 5, 61).

In Webster (Meiners, p. 17):
> *And let this brood of secure foolish mice* ·(*W. D.* 27 b).

In Middleton (Schulz, p. 26), but at the beginning of the verse:
> *Thou secure tyrant, yet unhappy lover* (I, 268).

In Jonson (Wilke, p. 42):
> *For this the secure dresser bade me tell* (*N. T. Prol.*).

apás, 4014. Cf. Oxf. Dict. under *apace*.

appérte, 688. Cf. Oxf. Dict. s. v.

avíssely, 3165. Cf. ib. s. *advisedly*.

enuýous, 2047:
> *Viscownte of Valewnce, enuyous of dedys*.

Cf. the accentuation of the subst. *envýe*: *Rom. of the Rose* 1653; *Monkes Tale*, 404; *King Horn*, 707, and Wissmann, *Q. F.* 16, p. 47.

c) in *Piers the Plowman*:

cóllateral, C 17, 285; B 14, 297. In Chaucer, *Troil.* I, 262: *col-láteràl*; also Barbour, *Bruce*, I, 56.

éntyreliche, C 11, 188.

íngrat, C 20, 219. So the modern stress, but cf. Scott, *Lord of the Isles* V, 2:

> *Of man ingrate and maid deceived.*

also Milton, *P. R.* III, 138, and subst. ib. 97.

párauenture, páraunter, párauntre, pér-auenture, B 5, 648; C 10, 180; B 11, 413; A 12, 8; B 12, 184; C 17, 50. In Chaucer with stress on the second syllable: *Hous of F.* 304: *Pard. T.* 935.

próphitable, A 7, 262. Cf. ten Brink § 287.

próuincials, próuyncial, A 8, 178; B 11, 56.

récreaunt, B 18, 100. Cf. p. 81 above.

bénygne, bénygneliche, B 12, 114; B 16, 7; B 18, 116. In Chaucer with stress on the second syllable. Cf. Oxf. Dict. s. v.

érraunt, C 7, 307. In Chaucer stress on the second syllable. Cf. Oxf. Dict. s. v.

órientales, B 2, 14. With French accentuation in Chaucer, *Leg.* 221.

sémblable, C 11, 157. With French accentuation in Chaucer, *Merch. T.* 256.

ýmaginatyf, ýmagynatyf, B 10, 115; B 12, 1. With stress on second and fourth syllables in Chaucer, *Frank. T.* 366.

a-pérteliche, apértly, B 3, 256; A 5, 15. Cf. p. 81 above.

depártable, B 17, 26; C 19, 189, 216; *in-depártable,* C 19, 27.

impárfit, inpárfit, inpárfyt, C 4, 389; C 12, 208; B 15, 50, 93; C 16, 136.

inmésurables, B 15, 69.

inpácient, B 17, 337.

inpóssible, B 10, 336.

d) in *Richard the Redeles*:

affórse, 4, 22. Cf. Oxf. Dict. s. v.

apárte, 4, 36. Cf. ib. s. v.

arére, 3, 110. Cf. ib. s. v.

Among the adjectives quoted above we meet with a considerable number in which the stress differs from that in Mod. E., and most of which have the accentuation of corresponding substantives or verbs. Words like *cónfus, ápparant, sécure,* were probably so stressed. The apparent accentuation *divine* in Shakspere, &c. may be explained by "hovering stress" ("schwebende Betonung"):

In Levins we find some remarkable deviations from our modern practice in the accentuation of adjectives:

éxcusable, 3, 21.

inéxcusable, 4, 23.

ínnumerable, 3, 29.

spirítual, 15, 22.

supernatúrall, 18, 40.

debónare, 29, 10.

défensory, 106, 43.

díuisible, 114, 4.

indíuisible, 114, 5 but

indiuísibil, 129, 19.

défective, 153, 13.

sátisfactóry, 107, 10.

dísiunctiue, 153, 31.

pérspectiue, 153, 37.

In Boyer also we find many deviations from modern use: *alternàte, áugust, béneficial, bénevolent, cháracteristick(al), chrómatick, circulatóry, compárable,* (but *incómparable*), *compárably* (adv.), *cómplaisant, compléx, concréte* (cf. Oxf. Dict.), *cónform* (adv.), *cónsummate* (cf. Oxf. Dict.), *cóntiguous, córrosive* (cf. Oxf. Dict.), *desperáte, desúltory, detrímental, etymólogical, exórable, fállacious, gallánt* (civil), *incómpatible, indúrate, irréfragabl{ᵉ/ᵧ, irrepréhensible* (but *irreprehénsibly*), *irréspectively* (adv.), *irrevócabl{ᵉ/ᵧ, lócomotive, máture, memorátive, modíficable* (obsolete), *palliátive, péradventure* (adv.), *pérennial, prófoundly* (but *profóund*), *protéstant* (and *The Protestánt Religion*), *quáternery, ràpacious, recitátive, recondìte, redólent, réfractory, retrogràde, revócable* (so also Encycl. Dict.), *rhùmatick, ridicúle,* ("an *Expression of no general Use, and about which Authors are divided"), splénetick* (cf. Encycl. Dict.), *stìgmatick, subaltérn, transvérse.*

In Bailey the following: *accéssorily* (adv. but *áccessory*, cf. Oxf. Dict.), *adorábly* (adv.), *adulátory, ámmoniac, análogical, avárous, áugust, cavérnous, centrifúgal, centripétal, cháotic, complaisánt* (cf. Oxf. Dict.), *compóund, concussíve* (printer's error?), *confíscate* (cf. Oxf. Dict.), *cónform, cónsolatory, contráry, contríte, convérsely* (adv.) (cf. Oxf. Dict.), *dedicátory, desperátely* (adv.), *desúltory, emánant, empyréal* (cf. Oxf. Dict.), *empyréan* (cf. Oxf. Dict), *exémplary* (cf. Oxf. Dict.), *explétive* (cf. Oxf. Dict.), *falsifíable, fecúnd, Hésperian, héxagonally* (adv.), *honórable* (but *honouráble*), *honórary* (and *hónorary*), *jéjune, imbécile, ináccessible, infámous, infuríate, ingráte* (cf. Encycl. Dict.), *intercálary, jovíal, irrevócable, isoscéles, jucúnd, juveníle, labórant, legíslative, matrónal, matutínal, mischíevous, mundáne, patrónal, phlégmatick, recóndite* (cf. Encycl. Dict.), *refléx* (so also Shakspere subst. *Rom.* III, 5, 20), *remédiless, revócable* (also subst. *revócableness*), *satúrnine, schísmatick, servíle, subaltérns, supplétory, tempestíve* (also adv. *tempestívely*), *transvérse, tripartíte, vavásory, viólable, unamíable, unprépossess'd, librátory.*

III. Verbs.

The verbs we group like the substantives, according the number of syllables, their composition and accentuation, and we separate obsolete words from those still in use.

1. Dissyllabic Verbs (including trisyllables with final unaccented e) with Prefix and modern Accentuation.

Among these we class also such verbs as are occasionally polysyllabic in their older forms. The majority of the verbs of this division usually leave the prefixes unstressed.

a) in the *Troy-Book*:

abásshet, 329, 2517.

abátede, 895.

abstéyne, 2600, 3386.

accépt, 4919.

accóunted, accóuntid, accóunttid, 586.

afférmyt, affírmet, affírmyt, 2675, 7847, 8420. 8869, 9693, 10476, 10620.

aiónet, aióyned, aióynet, aióynt, ajóynet, 128, 291, 350, 1135, 4154, 4565, 4947.

aiúgget, 4271, 4281.

anóyntide, 883.

appére, appérit, appérith, 1093, 1963, 4811, 2565, 4473.

appróche, apróchet, apróchit, apróchyt, 401, 1276, 6624, 6903, 7998.

aráyed, aráyit, 231, 750, 8478.

asáye, asáyet, 2489, 3903.

asséntid, asséntyd, 2103, 3122, 3191, 4241, 7204, 7862, 8945, 10475.

assígnet, assíngnet, 508, 969, 3449, 5193, 6089, 6107, 6215, 7383.

atíret, 5607.

cómford, 5429, 6587.

confóundit, 5905. Also with stressed prefix p. 90 below.

consáyuit, 13132. Also with stressed prefix p. 90 below.

cómpast, 496, 3056, 10292.

decláret, 2147, 2307, 3655, 4459. Also with stressed prefix p. 90 below.

delíted, 3951 With stressed prefix p. 90 below.

deményt, 3925.

denýet, 8494.

depértid, 1181, 2157, 3025, 4802, 7267.

désteynid, 2673.

dispíset, 5039.

dissáiue, 4445. With stressed prefix p. 91 below.

disséruyt, 12029. With stressed prefix p. 91 below.

distrácte, 3219.

distróy, distróyet, 28, 784, 3484, 9712.

enclíne, enclínet, enclýnet, 2245, 2305, 2448.

endúre, endúred, endúret, endúryng, 122, 207, 1336, 2661, 3465, 3529, 6534, 8415.

enfécte, 936.

enfórme, enfórmet, enfórmyt, enfóurmet, enfóurmyt, infórme, 652, 763, 770, 796, 809, 1497, 2639, 3011, 3223, 5111, 6186, 10039.

enióynit, 416.

enpáïre, enpáires, enpáyres, enpáyret, enpáyryng, impáiryt, 787, 2252, 2282, 3297, 3929, 4838, 8886.

exchéwe, 4910.

excúsit, 4910.

inclósede, 848.

obéy, obéyede, 135, 3672.

offéndit, 4209, 11164.

opprésse, oppréssed, opprésit, oppréssing, 3232, 3608, 4727, 5094, 5889, 7700, 7753, 7794, 7800, 7977, 9450, 9564, 9988, 10191 *redóundet,* 10183.

refrésshe, refrésshing, refrésshit, 338, 9115, 13327.

refút, 5723.

rcpréuet, repróued, repróuyt, 1817, 8473, 9545.

réscow, réskew, réskewet, 683, 7252, 8557, 9734, 10435.

resórt, 3553.

rcstóre, restóret, restóris, 1205, 1761, 1856, 2141, 4998, 5857, 7295, 10399.

sóiorne, sóiournet, 382, 2831. In this word, as in *réscow,* the
. prefix was no longer felt as sueh.

transláted, 71.

b) in the *Morte Arthure*:

abáischite, 255.

accórde, accórdide, 344, 3133.

acóunte, 405.

ajóurnede, 340.

a-júggede, 862. 1658, 3411, 4110.

alówe, alówes, 396, 1036.

appróches, 4105.

aréste, aréstede, 329, 633, 1429.

a-sáye, assáye, 2347, 2615, 4312.

ascénte, assénte, 644, 1506, 1963.

assíngnez, assíngnyde, 240, 727.

anóyeddyde, 2051.

cómforth, cómforthe, cómfurthe, cómfurthes, 696, 830, 944, 1839, 3131.

cónquerid, cónqueryd, cónqueryde, 24, 284, 402.

deménys, 1988, 4076.

enbráces, enbrássede, enbrássez, 1753, 2459, 2518, 4111.

enclésside, enclósede, enclósez, 1134, 2396, 4206.

enclíned, enclíncde, enclínes, 83, 479, 1706.

encróche, encróchede, encróchez, encróyssede, 1243, 2036, 3426, 3525, 4112.

endénte, endénttyd, 2052, 3297.

endíttede, 3420.

enféblesches, 2484.

enfórce, enfórsse, 225, 364.

enjóyne, cnjóynede, enjóynes, enjóynys, 445, 2087, 2897, 4109.

ensúre, 1689, 2324, 3734.

énteres, éntirde, éntire, éntrede, éntyrde, 1691, 1967, 2007, 2387, 3448, 4069.

escháɾpe, eschápede, escháppede, escháppide, 1117, 1881, 2367, 2957, 3576.

eschéue, eschéuede, eschéwede, eschéwes, 1116, 1539, 1620, 1750, 1881, 2956, 3000, 3027, 3347.

prófers, prófire, 1376, 2533, 2534, 3141.

ráunsound, ráunsounde, ráwnsone, ráunsonéde, 100, 293, 466, 1276, 1508, 2667, 3275.

réleuis, réleuyde, rélyede, rélyes, rélyez, 1391, 1882, 2234, 2278, 4291. These various forms have the meaning of the modern *rálly.* Cf. the accentuation in *P. P.* below.

réscewe, réscowede, 363, 1752, 2243, 4131.

sóiorne, sóiourne, súggeournez, súggeourns, súggourne, 54, 153, 354, 624, 1335, 4027, 4042. In Chaucer, *Compl. of Mars,* 78 *sojóurned.*

c) in *Piers the Plowman:*

a-báissed, abáisshed, abásched, C 7, 17; B 10, 286, 445; C 16, 163.

abáte, B 6, 218; A 7, 171.

a-córde, a-córded, a-córden, a-córdeth, a-córdynge, C 4, 358, 364, 374; A 5, 179; A 10, 87, 89; B 11, 42; B 20, 301; C 20, 285.

a-cóunte, acóunted, acóunteth, C 4, 396; C 8, 33; C 10, 239; B 11, 15, 127; C 11, 258; B 19, 410.

afróntede, C 23, 5.

aláyed, C 18, 79.

allówed, allóweth, a-lóweth, B 10, 433, 435; B 14, 307; B 15, 4.

aménde, B 1, 166; B 10, 269, 319.

amóunteth, A 3, 87.

anúyed, a-núyzed, anúyzen, A 2, 97, 144; A 3, 182; A 5, 74.

a-péiren, apéireth, C 4, 164; A 7, 158.

a-péredeth, A 1, 98.

appróched, B 18, 170.

aquíte, aquýte, C 16, 12; C 21, 394.

a-sáilen, assáilled, C 14, 63; B 18, 294.

a-scápie, C 4, 61.

assáye, assáyen, A 3, 5; C 9, 22; B 16, 74, 106; C 17, 164; B 18, 96.

a-swágen, A 5, 100.

a-táche, a-tácheth, A 2, 174; C 12, 306.

atéynte, B 20, 161.

auáilled, B 10, 273.

auáunce, B 9, 159.

auýse, B 15, 314.

a-vówe, a-vówed, C 7, 438; C 8, 13; C 16, 144.

cómpas, cómpassed, B 10, 178; B 19, 235.

confórmen, B 13, 213. Also with stressed prefix, p. 95.

cónseilleth, cóunseildest, cóunseile, cóunseilede, A 3, 180, 199; A 8, 182; A 10, 191; B 19, 109. Cf. the subst. p. 59. In Chaucer, *Wife of B. Prol.* 66, with stress on the second syllable.

defámed, de-fámeth, A 2, 138; A 11, 64.

defénde, deféndeth, B 16, 246; C 17, 135. Also with stress on the prefix p. 96 below.

defýed, defýen, A 5, 219; B 20, 65.

de-párte, A Pr. 78. Also with stressed prefix, p. 96 below.

depráue, A 3, 172; B 5, 144.

deschárget, dischárgen, A 4, 26; B 15, 528.

deséruet, A 7, 80. With stressed prefix pp. 91, 96 below.

dispíse, dispíseth, B 2, 79; B 15, 54.

embáumed, enbáumede, enbáwmed, C 14, 107; B 17, 70; C 20, 86.

encháunte, C 18, 288.

endíte, C 16, 119. With stressed prefix p. 96 below.

enfórme, enfóurmed, B 15, 548; B 17, 125.

engréynen, B 14, 20.

enióigned, en-ióynen, C 3, 150; B 14, 287.

ennúyed, B 5, 94.

enpúgnede, impúgned, inpúgned, inpúgnen, B Pr. 109; B 7, 147; B 13, 123; C 16, 131.

enséure, A 6, 31.

enspíreth, C 17, 243.

escháunges, B 5, 249.

expóunen, B 14, 277.

repréued, repróueth, C 4, 389; B 12, 138; B 17, 149.

tréspassed, A 3, 274; B 12, 284.

d) in *Richard the Redeles:*

abáted, abáteth, 3, 307; 4, 81.

acóuñted, acóuntid, 3, 155, 157.
agréued, 2, 113.
anóyed, 3, 71.
asséntid, 3, 109.
decláre, 1, 50.
endíted, 3, 63.
entént, enténte, Pr. 79; 2, 99.
recláyme, 2, 182.
rehérse, 4, 43.

The remark under *sóiorne,* p. 86, applies also to such verbs as *cómford, énter, prófers, ráunsound, cónseilleth, tréspassed.*

2. Dissyllabic Verbs (including Trisyllables with final unaccented *e*) with Prefix and with Accentuation differing from the present one.

The number of such verbs is not inconsiderable. The accented prefixes, with few exceptions, begin with consonants. The alliteration of the particles beginning with vowels (nearly all in *P. P.*) is often doubtful. Many of the accentuations that differ from those of the present day occur also in Chaucer and later poets.

a) in the *Troy-Book*:

cómaund, cómaundet, cómaundant, 271, 1175, 2548, 2557, 2564, 2750, 3517, 6210, 7109, 7192, 8534, 11175, 11397, 12681, 13002, 13025.

Cf. *Cleanness,* 1428; also in Oxf. Dict. the quotations from *Curs. Mund;* further in Middleton (Schulz, p. 23):
Of life and death, and cannot command case (I, 160)
and three more examples.

In Jonson (Wilke, p. 39):
Some commands. from you, lately, gentle lady (D. A. II, 25)
at the beginning of the verse. Cf. also Schipper II, 152, and the stress of the subst. p. 69 above.

cómendith, cómendyng, 10315, 11841. Cf. p. 95 below.
cómyn, cómynd, cómynt, cómonyng, cómyning, 502, 1003, 2939, 2964, 4023, 11318, 11336, 11428, 11597, 11711, 11721, 12046, 12298.

The stress of the verb *commune* still varies at present. Cf. Oxf. Dict. and examples there.

cómpilet, 53.

cónfermyt, *cónfirmit*, 2556, 7593, 8968. Cf. Shaksp. (König p. 74): *Which I will do with confirm'd countenance* (*M. A.* v. 3, 17). after the cæsura.

Webster (Meiners, p. 18): *To confirm patience in us: Your delays* (*D. L.* 119 a) at the beginning of the verse.

cónfound, 2333; with stress on second syllable, p. 85 above. Cf. Jonson (Wilke, p. 40): *To confound nature and to ruine that* (I, 72) *That confounds all. And makes a mungrill breed, father,* (*D. A.* II, 30) both at the beginning of the verse. Cf. also Schipper II, 152.

cónceyuit, *cónsaiued*, *cónsayuit*, 1230, 1256, 1918, 2039, 2513, 5135, 7191, 12758, 13232, 13854. With stress on second syllable, p. 85 above. Cf. the stress of the subst. p. 70 above.

cónsumet, 7151, 9531, 12289. Cf. Chapman (Elste, p. 31): *To consume all your hours in close retirements* (418 a) at the beginning of the verse. Jonson (Wilke, p. 40): *As we were onely bred to consume corne* (I, 691). after the cæsura. Cf. also Schipper II, 152.

déclaret, 4459. With stress on second syllable, pp. 85, 89 above. Cf. Jonson (Wilke, p. 40): *A declar'd cuckold on good termes? this pearle* (I, 511) at the beginning of the verse. *Your friend apparent you! You declar'd hell-hound* (*D. A.* II, 22) after the cæsura.

déliuer, 628. So also *Cleanness*, 500. In Chaucer with present stress.

délited, 3927, 3981. With stress on second syllable p. 85 above.

déuydyt, 7220. Cf. the accentuation of the adj. *díuisible*, *Man. Voc.* 114, 4. Also Middleton (Schulz, p. 24): *Shall diuide me from you, O faithful treasure* (I, 198) at the beginning of the verse.

déuys, déuysede, déuyses, 660, 4018, 4938. So also *Cleanness,* 1046. Subst. pp. 61, 63 above.

díssauis, déssauis, díssaiue, 743, 754, 11230. Cf. the subst. pp. 61, 62 above.

díssiret, díssirit, díssirond, díssyring, désyred, désyret, déssyret, déssyrit, díssyret, 478, 2221, 2971, 3603, 5122, 6415, 7897, 8883, 9457, 10502, 11493, 11651, 12478, 12707, 13372, 13800, 13866. Cf. Middleton (Schulz, p. 24):

    Lady, we have, and desire rather now (IV, 544)

after the cæsura.

dísseruet, 7901. With stress on the second syllable p. 88 above. Cf. the accentuation of the subst. p. 62 above. Also Schipper II, 152.

pérfourme, pérfourmet, 2022, 4172, 4220. Cf. Chapman (Elste, p. 32):

    To perform nothing, are like shallow streams (239 b)

at the beginning of the verse.

pérsauit, pérsauyt, pérsayuet, pérceyuit, 137, 677, 1771, 1815, 2047, 2875, 3103, 5010, 5814, 5867, 6397, 7315, 9262, 9429, 9436, 10341, 10363, 11240, 11403, 11421, 13517. Cf. the subst. *párceit* p. 76 above. Also the accentuation in Middleton (Schulz, p 25):

    I perceive then a woman may be honest (IV, 98)

    I perceive fools are not at all times foolish (IV, 524).

    In Jonson (Wilke, p. 41):

I perceive nothing with. I offer at nothing (D. A. II, 41)

all at the beginning of the verse.

présent, 2189, 9450, 11442, 11479, 12098. Cf. Webster (Meiners, p. 18):

    To present bribe in fist: the rest o'the band (WD. 28 b).

    Middleton (Schulz, p. 25):

    Can present to us, yet for truth's probation (III, 638)

both at the beginning of the verse.

prócure, prócur, prócour, próker, prókert, prókuryng, 5617, 9226, 11555, 11558, 11603, 11614, 13766. Cf. Jonson (Wilke, p. 41):

    And procure sweet and then procure a bath (I, 376)

    To procure moneyes for the needful charge (I, 701)

both at the beginning of the verse. Cf. also Schipper II, 152.

púrsew, púrsewis, púrsewit, púrsu, 1150, 3685, 7417, 7749, 7956,
9657, 12051. Cf. the accentuation of the noun, p. 61 above;
also in Webster (Meiners, p. 18), after the cæsura:
To safety in the camp. Some pursue the villain (*A. V.* 173 a).
In Middleton (Schulz, p. 26), at the beginning of the verse:
To pursue truth to death, if the cause rous'd in (IV, 381).
In Jonson (Wilke, p. 42):
In all their drifts and counsels pursue profit (I, 398).
Also the noun in Marlowe, but at the beginning of the
verse:
In pursuit of the city's overthrow (I, 50).
Cf. also Schipper, II, 152.

púruay, púruait, púruayet, púrueit, púrvey, 2132, 3252, 5365,
5395, 8819, 8858, 9379, 10576, 10648, 11700, 11898, 12771.
Cf. the accentuation of *purveyor* in Shakspere (König p. 74;
Abbot p. 396):
To be his purveyor: but he rides well (*M.* I, 6, 22)
and *púrviaunce,* p. 69 above.

réceyuit, résayuit, 5297, 8073, 12731. Cf. in Chapman (Elste,
p. 33), at the beginning of the verse:
To receive kindness, than from thee, an eunuch (428 b).
In Dekker (Kupka, p. 16), after the cæsura, and at the
beginning of the verse:
Had it for lesse than I, yet receiude more (III, 297)
Should receiue nourishment: for being the head (ib.).
In Middleton (Schulz, p. 26):
I tax his youth of common receiv'd riot (II, 335)
and three more examples.
In Jonson (Wilke, p. 42):
For they that win doe seldome receive shame (I, 718).
Cf. also Schipper, II, 152.

réleshe, 13626. Cf. the accentuation of the subst. *reles* p. 62
above, and Schipper, II, 152

rémeve, 5586. Cf. Webster (Meiners, p. 18), at the beginning
of the verse:
To remove forth the common hospital (*D. M.* 86 a).
Middleton (Schulz p. 26):
To place my name, that should have remov'd princes (IV, 309).

rénonse, 13629.

rétaynit, 10936. Cf. Webster (Meiners, p. 18):

> *Will seem a princely progress retaining* (*DM.* 80 a).

Middleton (Schulz, p 26), at the beginning of the verse:

> *And retain deadly follies in myselfi* (II, 334).

réstore, réstorit, 6572, 11201, 13087. In Chaucer with present accentuation:

> *That men the quene Eleyne shal restore,*
> *And Grekes us restore that is mis.* (*Troil.* IV, 1347, 8).

réwardet, 3876. Cf. the accentuation of the subst. pp. 61, 62 above, and in Middleton (Schulz, p. 26):

> *In others reward you and all your actions* (III, 581).
> *To reward virtue in him by this fortune* (III, 581).

súffices, súffis, súffise, súffises, 4457, 6747, 9356, 13332, 13609. *Pearl,* 135 and Chaucer have modern accentuation.

súppose, 2317. Cf. Chapman (Elste, p. 33):

> *I found her supposed mistress fast asleep* (298 b).

sústayn, 7179. In Chaucer with modern accentuation.

b) in the *Morte Arthure*:

cómande, cómandez, cómandyde, cómaunde, cómaundez, cómaundyd, cómmande, cómmaundez, cómmaundyde, 71, 156, 626, 839, 935, 1218, 1271, 1319, 1585, 1602, 1637, 2356, 2392, 4148. Cf. p. 89 above.

cónfoundez, cónfundez, 1245, 1922. Cf. p. 90 above.

cónfusede, 123. Cf. the adj. p. 79 above.

cónuaye, cúnvayede, 482, 1589, 1604. Cf. Jonson (Wilke, p. 40):

> *To convey letters. Nor no youths disguis'd* (*DA.* II, 18).

at the beginning of the verse.

counsáyles, 305. With modern accentuation p. 88 above.

déuysede, dévisede, dévyse, dévysed, dývysyde, 49, 2400, 3388, 3527, 3573. Cf. p. 91 above.

déuorande, 2054.

díscendis, 3250.

éntyce, 307:

> *To entyce the emperour to take ouere the mounttes.*

Here we might also assume *entýce* and *take* as the bearers of the alliteration and absence of the second rime-letter. In *Cleanness,* 1137, the word has the modern accentuation.

pérsayfede, pérsayfes, pérsayuede, 1631, 2811, 4224. Cf. p. 91 above.

pérsewede, pérsewes, púrsue, púrsuede, 1377, 1476, 2155, 2786, 4046. Cf. p. 92 above.

péruersede, 2786.

présente, 684. Cf. p. 91 above.

prófesside, 4013. Cf. the stress of the subst. p. 70 above; also Chapman (Elste, p. 31), at the beginning of the verse:

I profess husbandry, and will not play (55 b).

In Middleton (Schulz, p. 26):

There can come none: a profess'd abstinence (I, 138).
When I that profess'd war, am overthrown (III, 571).

In Jonson (Wilke, p. 42), after the cæsura:

Little know they that professe amitie (*V*. II, 201).

Cf. also Schipper, II, 152.

púrtrayede, 3607. Cf. Marlowe:

Well hast thou pourtrayed, in thy terms of life (I, 29).
Upon his brows was pourtrayed ugly death (I, 53).

púruayede, 1925, 2477, 2332. Cf. p. 92 above.

rébuke, rébukkede, rébuyked, rébuykede, rébuykkyde, rébuykyde, 1333, 1445, 1705, 2153, 2234, 2374, 4283. Cf. *Pearl,* 367, with modern accentuation.

réherse, réhersede, réhersene, réhersys, 1666, 3206, 3229, 3452. Cf. Middleton (Schulz, p. 26), at the beginning of the verse:

You rehearse miseries, wife—call the maid down (V, 91).

rémouede, rémowes, 1417, 1761. Cf. p. 92 above.

répent, répente, répenttes, 1332, 1392, 3894. Cf. the stress of the subst. pp. 68, 69 above.

réquit, 1680.

résaywe, 3587. Cf. p. 92 above.

réstreynede, 2041. Chaucer has the modern stress.

rétournes, 1395. Cf. in Shaksp. (König, p. 74), after the cæsura:

Commend me to my wife. I'll return consul (*Cor.* III, 2, 135).

In Middleton (Schulz, p. 26), at the beginning of the verse:

And return'd safe, he would have been a light. (III, 312)

and three more examples.

In Jonson (Wilke, p. 42), at the beginning of the verse:

I returne instantly. Most worthy Lord (1, 423)

and three more examples. Cf. also Schipper, II, 152.

réuenge, réuengyde, 1204, 3217.

réuerssede, réuersside, 2070, 3255.

réuertede, 2918.

súpprisede, súpprissede, súppryssede, súpprysside, 1420, 1845, 1951, 2616, 3797, 3986. In Chaucer *supprýsed, Troil.* III, 1184.

c) in *Piers the Plowman*:

cómaunde, cómaunded, cómaundede, cómaundet, cómaundeth, A 1, 20; A 2, 173; B 2, 206; A 4, 6, 8, 72; C 5, 195; B 6, 16; C 6, 195; B 11, 175; C 9, 230; B 13, 46; C 14, 78; B 19, 109, 358, 361; C 21, 255. Cf. p. 89 above.

cómende, cómended, cómenden, cómendit, B 4, 158; A 11, 286; B 12, 178; C 17, 285. Cf. Middleton (Schulz, p. 23): *Most impious epicures! We commend rather* (IV, 402). Cf. also the adj. *commendable,* Schipper, II, 155.

cónceiued, cónceyue, cónceyued, cónseiued, cónseyued, cónseyuet, A 7, 36; A 9, 48; A 10, 136; B 11, 332, 404; C 11, 212, 218; B 18, 129. Cf. p. 90 above.

cónfermed, cónfermede, B 10, 354; B 15, 449; C 15, 39. Cf. p. 90 above.

cónformye, cónfourme, cónfourmen, C 4, 401; B 11, 175; B 13, 208; B 15, 337. Cf. p. 88 above, also *confirm* and *conform* in the Oxf. Dict. The accentuation *cónfourme* also in *Cleanness,* 1067.

cónfounde, cónfoundet, C 6, 191; A 11, 93. Cf. p. 90 above.

cóniured, B 15, 14. Cf. Oxf. Dict. s. v.

cónsenteth, C 3, 90. Chaucer has the modern accentuation.

cónspire, cónspiret, A 11, 19; C 12, 80. In Chaucer and Gower with modern accentuation.

cónstreyne, C 6, 54. With stress on second syllable in Chaucer, *Cl. T.* 472 and in *Gaw. & Gr. Knt.* 1496.

cónstrue, cónstruen, cónstrueth, cónstruweth, A Pr. 58; B Pr. 144, B 2, 36; A 4, 128, 133; B 5, 426; A 8, 91, 135; B 14, 276; C 18, 110. Here the stress still varies at the present time. Cf. Oxf. Dict. s. v. Boyer has the form *cónster.* So also Bailey.

cóntreeude, cóntreue, cóntreued, cóntreuede, cóntreueden, B Pr. 118; C 1, 144; C 8, 39; B 10, 19, 177; A 12, 8; C 15, 73, 161; B 16, 137. Cf. Shaksp. (König, p. 74; Schmidt, p. 1413): *To do no contrived murder: I lack iniquity* (O. I, 2, 3).

Cleanness, 266 the same accentuation. In Gower, *Conf.*
III, 90 and *Rom. Rose*, 4249 the modern stress. Cf. Oxf. Dict.
contrive.

cónuerted, cónuerten, B 16,110; C 18,186; C 21,190. In Chaucer
modern stress. Cf. Oxf. Dict. s. v.

défende, défendeth, défendyth, A 6, 84; A 12, 19; B 15,19. With
stress on second syllable, p. 88. Cf. the accentuation of the
subst. p. 58 above.

départen, B 20,138. Cf. Jonson (Wilke, p. 40), at the beginning
of the verse:

To depart Rome. Which you by all sought meanes (I, 743).

With present accentuation, p. 88 above, also *Cleanness*, 396,
7677. *Holy Rood*, 143, 368. Cf. Schipper, II, 152.

dépose, C 18, 215.

déserued, déseruen, B 4, 178; C 17, 4. Cf. p. 88 above.

déspeir, C 10, 38. Cf. Chapman (Elste, p. 31):

For all this, I'll not despair of my wager (327 b)

*déstroye, déstroyede, déstroyeth, déstruyed, déstruyen, dístroye,
dístruieth, dístruye, dístruyeth*, A 10, 76; B 10, 330; C 10, 17;
A 11, 280; C 15, 22; B 16, 165; B 18, 155; C 18, 293. With
the same stress: *Cleanness*, 1160.

déuised, déuyse, B 19, 273, 326. Cf. p. 91 above.

dílytede, A 1, 29. Cf. p. 90 above.

dísputyng, A 9, 108. Cf. ten Brink § 292; also the varying
stress of the modern *(in)disputable.*

díuide, dýuyde, B 19, 210, 234. Cf. p. 90 above.

éncombre, B 19, 223. In Chaucer with modern accentuation.
Cf. *cómbraunce*, p. 76 above.

éndited, B 11, 307. With stress on second syllable, p. 88 above.

éntisedest, éntysing, B 13, 322; C 21, 318. Cf. p. 93 above.

éxcepte, B 15, 274. Cf. Jonson (Wilke, p. 40):

The common monster, love, shall except thee (V. II, 205).

Cf. also Schipper, II, 152.

éxcused, B 17, 90. Cf. the stress of the adj. *inéxcusable, Man.
Voc.* 4, 23.

párceyued, párceyueth, pérceyue, pérceyue, B Pr. 100; B 5, 143;
B 13, 85, 301; B 15, 193; B 16, 23, 103; B 17, 66, 150; B 18,
241, 418; B 19, 158. Cf. p. 91 above.

párforme, párfourned, párfourneth, pérformede, pérformen, pér-forneth, pérfourneth, B 5, 405; A 6, 88; C 7, 283; C 8, 72; B 13, 78, 412; B 14, 290; C 14, 93; B 15, 320, 483; C 16, 173. Cf. p. 91 above.

pérmute, pérmuten, C 3, 185; B 13, 110. Cf. the stress of the subst. p. 70 above.

pórtrey, púrtraye, púrtreye, B 3, 62; B 15, 176; C 20, 136. Cf. p. 94 above.

présented, B 19, 88. Cf. p. 92 above.

présumed, B Pr. 108. Cf. the stress of the subst. p. 68 above.

púrsue, pórsuede, púrsewede, púrsued, púrsueth, B 3, 240; B 11, 14, 61, 180; B 12, 241; C 12, 176; B 17, 302; C 18, 167; B 19, 158, 428; C 19, 166. Cf. p. 92 above.

púrueye, B 14, 18. Cf. p. 92 above.

rébuke, rébuked, rébuken, B 5, 371; C 6, 82; B 11, 126, 363, 419. Cf. p. 94 above.

réceyue, réceyued, réceyuen, C 5, 196; C 6, 67; B 15, 502; B 17, 177, 185, 190; C 18, 42; B 19, 254. Cf. p. 92 above.

récorded, récorden, B 4, 157; C 5, 29; B 15, 601; B 18, 197, 328. Cf. Shaksp. (König, p. 72):

To be spoke to but by the recorder (R^3 III, 7, 30).

réfuse, réfused, réfusede, réfusy, C 4, 369; C 14, 233; B 17, 177; B 19. 365. Cf. in Chapman (Elste, p. 32), at the beginning of the verse:

To refuse mine for her; I pray look here (79 a).

In Jonson (Wilke, p. 42):
If I refuse. I will not refuse, brother (I, 957).

Cf. also Schipper, II, 152.

réherce, réherced, réhercen, réhersed, réhersede, réherside, B Pr 184; A 1, 22; A 4, 134, 145; A 5, 43; B 5, 182; A 11, 202; B 11, 405; C 13, 35; C 18, 25. Cf. p. 94 above.

réioyse, B 15, 499.

réleue, B 7, 32; C 14, 70; C 17, 314.

relýed, B 20, 147, with the meaning *rally.* Cf. p. 87 above.

répent, répente, répenten, répentenden, répenteth, A 5, 186; C 11, 52; B 12, 250; B 17, 235; B 19, 365. Cf. p. 94 above.

réwarded, réwarden, réwardeth, réwarding, B Pr. 127; C 4, 311;

C 6, 32; B 11, 129, 361; B 12, 209; B 14, 145, 148, 156, 168; B 19, 188. Cf. p. 93 above, and ten Brink, § 292.

súfficeth, súffise, súffiseth, C 5, 12; B 17, 31; C 18, 119. Cf. p. 93 above.

d) in *Richard the Redeles*:

cónstrew, cónstrewe, cónstrewed, cónstrwe, Pr. 72; 1, 83; 3, 35, 327; 4, 68. Cf. p. 96 above.

córrette, Pr. 59. In Chaucer with modern accentuation. Cf. *córectoures,* p. 71 above.

dísceyued, 2, 111. Cf. p. 91 above.

díspise, 3, 199. With modern stress, pp. 85, 88 above.

dísplese, 2, 70. *Patience,* 1, with modern stress.

prónouncid, 4, 36. In Chaucer, *Troil.* IV, 213, with modern stress.

rébuke, rébuked, 3, 221, 340. Cf. pp. 94, 97 above.

réffourmed, Pr. 21. *Sir Gaw.* 377 and Gower, *Confi* I, 273 have modern stress.

réhersid, 2, 98; 3, 315. Cf. pp. 94, 98 above.

rémeveth, 3, 301. Cf. pp. 93, 94 above.

répreue, 3, 197. Cf. the stress of the subst., p. 63 above.

The numerous examples of verbs with accented prefix, like *cómaund, cónsume, dísyre,* &c. cannot be set aside by the assumption that they are instances of metrical errors. It is true, the quotations from Shakspere, &c. prove little for such an accentuation, as most of those verbs occur either at the beginning of the verse, or immediately after the cæsura, and such apparent accentuations occur also in modern poets, as for instance in Browning (*Ferishtah,* p. 33):

> *Pain deserved nowhere by the common flesh,*

in Arnold (*Merope,* p. 373):

> *To receive Arcas, who to-day should come.*

Yet the considerable number of such accentuations in the alliterative poets, and syncopated forms like *comse,* force on us the conclusion that they really had such stress in the spoken language. A direct proof of this for early Mod. E. we find again in Levins, *Man. Voc.*:

to ábsent, 66, 46.

to áccent (accinère), 66, 4.

to díuest, 82, 33.
to déstil, 126, 38.

From Boyer's *Dictionary* too we have to record deviations from modern accentuation:

àpply, áttract, cóllate, commúne (the stress still varies at the present time, cf. Oxf. Dict. s. v.), *cónjoyn, cónsent, cóntract* (*"passer contrat"* but *contráct, "abréger"*), *décamp, déter* (but also *detérr*), *emblém*, (*énthrall*), *érect, pórtend, pórtray, prólong*. From Bailey's *Dictionary*: *ábsent, árray, récoin*.

3. Dissyllabic Verbs (including Trisyllables with final unstressed *e*) without Prefix and with modern Accentuation.

a) in the *Morte Arthure*:
fórraye, fórrayede, fórrayse, 1247, 2489, 3019.
méruailles, 1314.

b) in *Piers the Plowman*:
cóueite, cóueited, cóueiten, cóueitest, cóueiteth, cóueyte, cóueyted, cóueyten, cóueytest, cóueyteth, A 3, 254; C 4, 255, 365; A 6, 63; A 8, 52; A 9, 103; A 10, 98, 191; B 10, 338; C 10, 193; A 11, 207; B 11, 10, 120; B 15, 39; B 18, 167; B 20, 252.
édefyen, édifye, C 10, 203; B 16, 132.
meynténe, B 13, 125.

4. Dissyllabic Verbs (including Trisyllables with final unstressed *e*) without Prefix and with Accentuation differing from the present one.

a) in the *Troy-Book*:
máintene, máintenede, máyntene, 2049, 8940, 9326, 9736. Cf. in Shaksp. (König, p. 74; Abbot, p. 394):
And maintain such a quarrel openly (*Tit.* II, 1, 47)
That here you maintain several factions (*H*[6] I, 1, 71).
In Jonson (Wilke, p. 41):
Must maintaine manly, not be heard to sing (*H.* II, 13).

In the first and last of these quotations, however, the word occurs at the beginning of the verse.

órdainet, 3338. With the same stress in *Will. of Pal.* 3791.
sálut, sálute, 392, 1909. In Chaucer: *saléweth (Shipman's Tale*
94); *saléwed (Frankl.'s T.* 582).

b) in the *Morte Arthure:*

máyntene, máyntenyde, 399, 4278.
órdaine, órdaynede, 661, 1991.
sáluʒed, sáluʒede, sáluʒ, 82, 87, 953.
tóurmentez, túrmentez, túrmenttez, 824, 842, 1954, 3153. Cf. the
accentuation *túrmentours,* p. 75 above.

c) in *Piers the Plowman:*

déuine, déuinede, déuyne, déuyne, déuyned, déuynede, díuinede,
B Pr. 209; B 7, 157; A 8, 138; A 11, 138; C 11, 99, 101; C 12,
265; B 13, 89; B 15, 589; B 19, 234. Cf. the subst. p. 73 above.
méynteyneth, méyntene, méynteneth, A 2, 171; B 2, 37; A 3, 160,
178, 209, 232; A 4, 42; C 18, 234.
órdeigne, órdeyne, órdeynede, C 18, 16; B 19, 315, 317.

d) in *Richard the Redeles:*

ménteyned, méynetene, 3, 311, 354.
órdeyne, órdeyned, 3, 204, 213.
    In Levins: *to póllute,* 196, 20.
    In Boyer: *to vácate, mólest(ed).*

5. Verbs of three or more Syllables with Prefix and modern Accentuation.

a) in the *Troy-Book:*

óccupiet, 5329.
appáreld, 3337.
assémble, assémblet, assémblid, assémblit, 85, 1034, 1176, 1277,
1289, 1309, 2571, 2576, 2983, 4577, 5160, 5774, 6073, 6739,
6758, 7108, 7117, 7556, 7860, 10135, 10281, 10671. With
different accentuation (?) p. 102 below. Cf. the subst. p. 65
above.
delíuer, delíuert, delýuer, 3958, 5337, 8611, 7903, 10024, 13756.
With prefix stressed, p. 102 below.

detérmynet, 2392.
disfígurt, 8524.
disséuert, 1602.
dissmémbrit, 3488.
enábit, 101, 110, 2856, 2858. Cf. Lawrence, pp. 76, 77.
engéndres, engéndreth, 3596, 7959.
exámynt, 3193. Not quoted by Lawrence.

b) in the *Morte Arthure*:

ócupyes, 1663, 2360.
appáirelles, appáyrellde, appáraylle, 500, 2461, 3365.
assémble, assémbles, 1578, 1852, 1962, 3788.
discóueres, 1641, 3119.
disséuere, disséuerez, disséueride, 1575, 1978, 3529.
dysfégoures, 2769.
enámelede, enámelde, ennélled, 1294, 2027, 2565, 3355. Cf.
    Lawrence, p. 63 sq.
encónters, encóntre, encóntrede, encóuntire, encóuntere, 1185,
    1320, 1787, 2158, 3491, 4180.
engénderde, engéndure, 843, 3743.
enuérounde, envérounes, enuérownde, envérounde, 2051, 2094,
    3242, 4124.

c) in *Piers the Plowman*:

cónterfeteth, cóunterfeten, A 11, 19, 133.
óccupied, óccupien, B 5, 409; B 16, 196.
réuerenced, réuerencede, réuerences, réuerenceth, C 10, 123, 191;
    C 14, 248; C 15, 182; B 16, 226; B 18, 256; B 19, 69.
amórtesed, B 15, 315.
a-páraile, appárayled, A 6, 7; A 7, 53.
delýuered, C 14, 41.
encómbred, encómbreth, encómbry, en-cómbrye, C 2, 67, 192; C 15,
    17; C 22, 220. With stressed prefix, p. 96.
engéndrede, engéndrure, A 7, 219; C 11, 215.
en-hábiten, C 10, 188.
rekéuered, B 19, 156.

d) in *Richard the Redeles*:

detérmyned, 2, 97.

6. Verbs of three or more Syllables with Prefix and with Accentuation differing from the modern one.

a) in the *Troy-Book*:

ássembled, 8903:
> We hade ass(em)eld ben at Attens, all oure ost Somen.

Quoted by Lawrence as an example of the alliteration *a.a:o.* We might also assume absence of first rime-letter.

áunterede, áunterid, áuntert, áuntrid, 314, 724, 742, 1831, 1899, 2107, 2543, 2783, 2862, 3179, 3269, 4125, 4181, 5479, 5770, 6376, 6617, 6796, 7006, 7122, 7245, 7254, 7306, 7532, 7676, 7761, 7766, 7778.

Classed here, among trisyllables, on account of the fuller form *aventure.* Cf. the accentuation of the subst. p. 67, and of the adj. p. 78.

cónsider, cónsidered, cónsidirs, cónsidret, 268, 2238, 2714, 4155.
In Chaucer, *Leg.* 225, 408, with modern accentuation.

cóntynu, 7419. Cf. the adv. p. 78 above, and Schipper, II, 158.

recóunseld, 12931, is the modern *reconcile,* but with the sense of *recover.* The accentuation was probably caused by imaginary connection with *counsel.*

b) in the *Morte Arthure*:

ánters, áunter, áuntyre, áwnters, áwntrende, 360, 1498, 1596, 1660, 1967, 2007, 2717.

délyuerede, 1688. With stress on second syllable, p. 101 above. In *Cleanness* the accentuation varies: with second syllable stressed: 1084; first syllable stressed: 500. So also *Pearl* 652.

rémembirde, 3892. Chaucer has modern stress. Cf. also the subst. p. 70 above.

c) in *Piers the Plowman*:

áuntred, áuntreth, C 11, 216; B 18, 220.

cóntinue, C 6, 104.

délyure, B 16, 266.

désauowe, C 4, 322.

dísalowed, B 14, 130.

dísconfit, C 1, 108. Chaucer, *Kn. T.* 1861, has the stress on the second syllable. Cf. *skómfitoure,* p. 66 above.

énuenymes, énuenymeth, B 2, 14; B 12, 256. The second of these verses has faulty alliteration:
And alle the other ther it lyth· enuenymeth thorgh his attere.

In Chaucer, *Wife of Bath, Prol.* 474: *envenýme; Monk's T.* 134: *envénimed; March. T.* 816: *envéniminge.*
récomendeth, B 15, 228.

From verses like Chaucer's, *Sec. Nonne's T.* 544:
To récoménde to yów, er thát I gó,
no conclusion can be drawn for such an accentuation.
réconforted, B 5, 287. In Chaucer *récomfòrte.*

In Levins *Man. Voc.* we find the following examples
énterlace, 7, 25.
récommend, 66, 22.
·cómprehend, 66, 23.
réprehend, 66, 24.
díscontinew, 95, 15.

There also *recógnise,* 148, 23, where we now stress the prefix.

From Boyer we quote the following accentuations:
advertìse, compénsate, condéscend, contémplate (in which the stress still varies, cf. Oxf. Dict. s. v.), *cóunter-mand, disàbuse, éradicate, miscónstrue, misémploy, prógnosticate, reconcíl{ᵉ_ing.*

From Bailey: *advertíse, ascértain, confiscáte, constéllated* (cf. Oxf. Dict.), *emígrate, epicúrize, excávate, interpólate, miscónstrue* (cf. Encycl. Dict.), *reconcíle, sulordináte, peregrínate.*

Johnson has: *advertíse, compénsate, constéllate, miscónstrue, reconcíle.*

7. Verbs of three or more Syllables, without Prefix and with modern Accentuation.

Of these we have no examples to record from our texts.

8. Verbs of three or more Syllables, without Prefix and with Accentuation differing from the modern one.

In *Piers the Plowman:*
ýmagenen (?), cf. the remark under *inwit,* p. 17, *ýmagyned* (?), B 13, 289, 358. In Chaucer the word has the modern stress.

In Levins only *séquester*, 83, 26.

In Boyer: *gésticulate, variegate.*

In Bailey: *articled, habituáte, patroníze, temporíze.*

9. Dissyllabic obsolete Verbs.

Under these we class also verbs with final unaccented *e*.

a) in the *Troy-Book*:

cónnse, 2065. This form proves the older accentuation of *commence*. Cf. Oxf. Dict. s. v. In Chaucer the syncopated form does not occur.

cómbir, cómburt, cumbrit, 2065, 4214, 11331, 11759. Cf. the remark under *cumber* in Oxf. Dict.

córonyd, 5381. In Chaucer, *Monkes T.*, 374, we find the accentuation *coróuned*. The ME. syncopated form *crunen* shows that also the second syllable was stressed. Cf. *crown* in Oxf. Dict.

affórce, 228. Cf. Oxf. Dict. s. v., and the adv. p. 83 above.

affráy, affráyet, 1084, 3200, 8429. Still found in Mod. E. poets. Cf. Oxf. Dict.

anóisyt, 220.

aspíes, 4574. So also Chaucer, *Pard. T.* 755.

auéntid, 7092. Cf. Oxf. Dict. s. v.; also *avéntaile*, p. 77 above.

The following also leave the prefix unstressed:

defóulede, defóules, 2475, 5091. Quoted here on account of the Romance prefix.

degráted, 12576. Cf. *degrade* in the Oxf. Dict.

deráyne, 13084. Cf. the syncopated form *dreinen* in Stratm.-Bradl.

repúgnet, 2670. Also in Spenser and Shakspere.

b) in the *Morte Arthure*:

auántid, aváuntede, 1594, 2864. The first of these verses runs:

At euene at his awene borde auantid his lordez.

Here, as in 2864, we have probably to stress the second syllable. By Lawrence this verse is not quoted. Chaucer, *Wife of B.*, 158, also accents the second syllable.

réhetede, réhetes, réhetez, 221, 411, 3198. In the *Rom. of the Rose*, 6509, *rehéte*.

rélayes, 1529. The word is not found in Stratm.-Bradl.

rénayede, 2913, 3572, 3892. So also *Cleanness,* 105. *Patience,* 344. Chaucer accents the second syllable.

répendez, 2107. An OFr. *rependre* is not given in Godefroy. In Stratm.-Bradl. the word does not occur. According to the Gloss. Index, it means "hang back".

réueste, 4334. Chaucer, *Troil.* III, 353, accents the second syllable.

abáiste, abáyste, 1423, 3737. Cf. *abase* and *abash* in the Oxf. Dict.; also Gloss. Index to *E. E. All. Poems: abayst.*

affráye, affráyede, 2804, 3226. Cf. p. 104 above.

aráse, 4098. Cf. *arace* in the Oxf. Dict.

avíres, 3164. Cf. Oxf. Dict. s. v.

defádide, 3304. Cf. Oxf. Dict. s. v.

enbúschede, enbúschide, 1403, 1712. For form and stress cf. *ambush* in the Oxf. Dict.

endórdide, 199. Cf. *endore* in the Oxf. Dict.

enflúreschit, 198.

cngýste, 445.

enpóysone, 213.

ensége, enségede, enségge, 441, 1337, 1696.

ensérches, 2466, 4311.

For all these verbs cf. the Oxf. Dict.

c) in *Piers the Plowman*:

cómsed, cómsede, cómseth, cúmse, cúmseth, A 1, 128, 139; C 5, 24; B 6, 316; A 9, 16; A 10, 98; B 11, 395; B 12, 278; B 16, 75; B 18, 57; C 22, 97. Cf. p. 104 above.

cóngeyde, cóngeye, cóngie, A 3, 167; C 5, 195; B 13, 198. "Formerly stressed *congéy*" Oxf. Dict. s. v. Cf. Chaucer, *Troil.* V, 479 *congéyen.*

réclused, C 5, 116. In Stratm.-Bradl. only this passage quoted.

récrayed, B 3, 257. Cf. Skeat's Gloss. Index s. v.

réneye, B 11, 121, 125.

réuested, C 6, 112.

tránsuersed, tránsuerseth, C 4, 449; B 12, 234.

a-clóye, C 21, 296. So also Chaucer, *Parlem.* 517.

acóuped, B 13, 459.

afáiten, afáytyng, affáite, affáiteth, afféyteth, B 6, 32; C 7, 7; C 10, 170; B 11, 375; B 14, 296.

alóse, C 20, 101. So also Chaucer, *Troi.* IV, 1473; *Cleanness* 274.

apáied, a-páyed, A 7, 101; C 10, 178; C 16, 63. So also Chaucer.

a-póse, a-pósede, appósed, appóseden, A 1, 45; A 8, 127; A 12, 8;
B 13, 222; C 16, 93; C 17, 163.

a-sóile, asóyle, asóyled, a-sóylen, assóile, A Pr. 69; A 3, 41, 139;
C 13, 7; B 19, 185.

aspíe, aspíed, a-spíen, aspýed, A 2, 201; B 17, 32; B 19, 297;
C 22, 342.

asséale, assélen, A 2, 37; A 3, 143.

assérued, B 12, 197.

auáuntyng, C 7, 35.

For all these with the prefix *a-* cf. the Oxf. Dict.

defóuled, defóulen, defóuleth, A 2, 136, 138; C 4, 192; A 11, 60;
B 14, 23; B 15, 496. Cf. p. 104 above.

discréue, discríue, A 5, 62, 107; C 21, 214. So also in Chaucer.

enbláunched, B 15, 113.

endáuntede, C 18, 171.

engýned, B 18, 250. So also in Chaucer and Gower. Cf. Oxf.
Dict. s. v.

méynprise, C 5, 173. Cf. the subst. p. 76. In *Gamelyn,* 744,
the verb has the stress on the second syllable.

repúgnen, C 1, 136. Cf. p. 104 above.

d) in *Richard the Redeles*:

cómsith, 3, 190.

endáuntid, 3, 127, 351.

discrýue, 1, 23.

10. Trisyllabic obsolete Verbs.

a) in the *Troy-Book*:

dísusent, dýsasent, dýssaisent, 7849, 8016, 9369.

dístitur, 728.

astóneide, astónyet, astónyt, 1319, 2520, 3540.

b) in *Piers the Plowman*:

cóntreplede, cóntrepleide, cóntrepleteth, cóuntreplede, cóuntrepleide,
C 1, 138; C 9, 53, 88; B 12, 100; B 20, 382. Cf. *cóuntreplèted*
Chaucer, *Leg.* 479. Cf. also Oxf. Dict. s. v.

cóuntresegge, C 12, 224. Rom. prefix + Germ. verb. Cf *countersay* in Oxf. Dict.

éntermeten, éntermetyng, B 11, 406; B 13, 291. The second of these examples is verb. subst. Cf. *entermete* in Oxf. Dict. With verb stressed: *enterméted,* B 11, 408.

acómbre, acómbred, acómbreth, B 1, 194; B 2, 50; B 12, 57; B 19, 215.

a-máysterd, a-máystren, A 2, 117, 124; A 7, 200.

apóysende, apóysoned, A 3, 123; B 15, 523.

a-résonede, arésonedest, B 12, 218; C 14, 129, 184.

c) in *Richard the Redeles*:

acómbrede, acómbrid, 2, 28; 4, 67.

astónyed, 2, 8.

In the examples of the accentuation of words of Romance origin, which we have collected from our texts, and arranged in the preceding pages, it seems, at the first glance, as if no definite principle of accentuation could be recognised. On a closer examination, however, we can trace a certain regularity in the stressing of such words, and certain principles and reasons that seem to underlie that accentuation.

We shall therefore endeavour, in the following remarks, to indicate what seem to us to be the grounds on which the accentuations in our examples are based, and for this purpose we shall again, in our examination, distinguish between Substantives and Verbs.

I. Taking, in the first place, dissyllabic Nouns + Prefix, we notice that the accent is more frequently placed on the prefix. This is what might have been expected, and in accordance with the accentuation of nominal compounds of Germanic derivation. Just as we find, of Germanic words, *foreward, afterwarde, forwise* etc. stressed on the first syllable, in the same way Romance words like *cómpas, prélate, próloge, rélikes,* etc. have the accent on the prefix. In some instances this accentuation is confirmed also by the peculiar form of the word, as, e. g. *cóntek, cóndyth, díssyre, súbarbe, súrcotte.* But by the side of this Germanic accentuation, we also meet with cases, although less frequently, in which the original

French accent has been preserved, e. g. *defáute, defénce, dispíte, redrésse,* etc. This prevalence of stressed prefix shows itself not merely in a single alliterative poet, but it is a feature common to all of them.

And here we may perhaps exhibit, as it were in a statistical manner, what is the practice of our alliterative poets in the treatment of each separate prefix.[1])

mis, mes.

Although in the English prefix *mis* the accentuation varied, the Romance *mes* has the stress in our examples. So we find *míschefe, mýschefe, (T), mýschefe (M), méschaunce (L)*

e + s + consonant.

Our only example with parasitic *e* is *estate.* We find **astáte* and *ástate (T),* each occurring four times, and **estáte (L)* once.

a, ad.

Examples: *áccesse (L. 1), *assént (T.* often), **assáwtte (M. 3), *assétz (L. 1), *afféres (L. 1), *apéel (L. 3), *alárme (L. 1).* Boyer and Johnson have *accéss.* Johnson: *assént,* Bailey: *ássent.* Boyer has *áquests.*

ab.

Example: *ábsens (M. 1), *absénce (M. 1), *absérts (T. 1).*

con, com.

Examples: *cómford (T. 4), cómpas (T. 4), cómplaint (T. 3), *compláint (T. 2), cóndethe (M. 5), cóntek (M. 3), cóunsail (M. L.* often).

Levins accents: *contráct;* Boyer: *commént, concépt, concért, cónsult, contrást;* Bailey: *concréte, contóur, contrást;* Johnson: *cómment,* (v. & n.), *cóncert, cóncrete, cóntrast, cónsult (consúlt).*

de.

Examples: *défense (T. 13), déuyse (T. 1; L. 1), déceyte (L. 1), díssait (= deceit, T.* often), *désert (L. 1), *defáute (T. 1; M. 1; L. 2), délites (T. 3), *delýte (L. 1), *degré (T. 1; M. 1), díssyre, désyre (T.* often), *dýspaire (L. 1), *dispíte (T. 2; M. 1; L. 1).*

---

[1]) *T. = Troy-Book; M. = Morte Arthure; L. = Langland.* The figures after these letters indicate the number of times the word quoted occurs. The asterisk shows unstressed prefix.

dis.

Example: *dísseese* (*T.* 2), *dispéns (*M.* 1).

en, in.

Examples: *enquéstes (*L.* 1), *enténte, *inténs (*T.* often; *L.* 2).

Boyer has *invóice;* Bailey: *engíne, ingréss, invóice;* Johnson: *éngine, íngress, ínvoice.*

es, ex.

Examples: *íssue* (*L.* 1), *escháunge (*T.* 1), *assáy (*L.* 1).

Bailey accents: *exíle,* Johnson: *éxile.*

ob, of.

Example: *offénce (*T.* 1).

re.

Examples: *rélikes* (*T.* 1), *ráunsone* (*M.* 1), *réscowe* (*M.* 1), *rémcnaunt* (*M.* 1), *réscowe* (*M.* 4), *récorde* (*L.* 1), *réward* (*T.* 3; *L.* 2), *rénoun* (*M.* 1; *L.* 1), *réles* (*L.* 1), *répast* (*L.* 1), *répreff* (*L.* 1), *réscyte* (*L.* 1), *redrésse (*T.* 2), *repréfe (*T.* 1), *relíkkes (*M.* 1).

Bailey and Boyer have: *recórd,* Johnson accents on either syllable.

pro.

Examples: *próloge* (*T.* 2), *prófyre* (*M.* 1), *prophéte (*L.* 1), *púrsuet* (*T.* 2).

In Boyer we find *porténts*, in Bailey *prodúce*, in Johnson *porténts*, *próduce* (but he quotes Dryden for *prodúce*).

pre.

Examples: *prélates* (*T.* 1), *présent* (*L.* 1).

Boyer has *prétence*, Bailey: *precínct, preságe*, Johnson: *precínct, preságe, preténce.*

sub.

Examples: *súbjects* (*T.* 1), *súbarb* (*M.* 2), *subárbes (*M.* 1).

sur.

Examples: *súrcotte* (*M.* 2), *súrfet* (*L.* 1).

Bailey and Johnson have *survéy.*

tres.

Example: *tréspas* (*L.* 1).

Of obsolete nouns: *affráy (*T.* 2; *M.* 1), *avów (*M.* 3), which follow the accentuation of the verbs *affráyen, avówen;* and *dyspéns (*M.* 1).

Various causes may be indicated that have brought about this condition of things.

1. In some of our compounds the meaning of the prefix had become obscured, or its force was no longer understood, as, for example, in *issue, ráunsone, cóunsail,* etc., in which the stress on the prefix is indeed quite natural.

2. In many cases of compound nouns the corresponding uncompounded term is not found in English, or, when it occurs, has no allied meaning. Such compounds are:

ábsens, áccesse.
cómford, cómpass, cóndethe, cóntek.
déuyse, déceyt, désert, délites, dísyre.
próloge, prófyre.
prélates, présent.
rémenaunt, réscowe, récord, réward, rénoun, réles, répast, répref,
    rédresse, résceyte, rélikes.
súbjects, &c. &c.

But with unaccented prefix:
abséns.
assént, assáwte, assétz, afféres, apéel.
dispíte.
enténte.
offénse.
prophéte, &c.

In the great majority of these words the prefix is accented. Among those with unstressed prefix, the greater number of the prefixes begin with vowels.

In this connection it is, naturally, difficult to ascertain in how far the force or meaning of the prefix was still felt at the time of our alliterative poets. The prefix might still be recognised as such:

a) In words in which the Latin etymon was still sufficiently transparent, that is to say, for those who had received a learned education.

b) By reason of a knowledge of French.

On the other hand the accentuation of some older loan-word might be influenced by Continental French.

c) Finally, the force of the prefix would in most cases be entirely unrecognised as such among the uneducated classes, with the result that words thus compounded would assume the English accentuation.

3. The prefix would mostly remain unaccented in those words in which it was apparently meaningless, as in

> *eschaunge* (*change*)
> *defaute* (*faute*)
> *complaint* (*plaint*)
> *enqueste* (*queste*).

4. Hence unrecognised and unaccented prefixes could be dropped, e. g.

> *dispite* and *spite*
> *ensaumple* and *saumple*
> *astate* and *state*
> *defence* and *fence* &c. &c.

Indeed, as Behrens notices (*Franz. Lehnwörter im ME.*, 1886, p. 64), "apheresis, which is not unknown in continental Old French dialects, or in the Romance languages generally, is specially characteristic of French loan-words in ME."

For additional examples the reader is referred to the work quoted, where also instances are given of apheresis in Anglo-Norman, such as *pelé* for *appelé*.

In Mod. Engl. too, instances of apheresis are not rare (cf. Mätzner, *Engl. Gram.* I, p. 164), e. g. *sport* for *disport*, *prentice* for *apprentice*, *censer* for *incenser*.

The peculiarity of Engl. pronunciation of French, shown in this and the following section, may be explained chiefly by the fact that the unstressed part of the word (mostly a prefix) which preceded the accented radical part, was no longer understood, and so became meaningless or weakened in force. Hence, according to the practice in words of English derivation, this part could be dropped, in the same way as the English particles *y-, a-, be-* &c. (Cf. Morsbach, *ME. Gram.* § 69.)

5. Many substantives have the same accentuation as their corresponding verbs by which the stress of the former may have been influenced.

Examples:

defense (defenden),
eschaunge (eschaungen),
deceit (deceiven),
assent (assenten),
dyspair (dyspairen),
offence (offenden),
delyt (delyten),
desyr (desyren),
array (arrayen),
arest (aresten),
avys (avysen),
avow (avowen),

6. The distinction made by some writers between lighter and heavier prefixes serves no practical purpose as a guide towards an explanation of the accentuation of compounds. Sometimes, indeed, we find a so-called lighter prefix unstressed, and, on the other hand, a heavier one without the accent. Besides, where is the line to be drawn between those two kinds of prefixes?

7. Finally, the similarity between some English and Romance prefixes has no doubt exerted an influence on the accentuation of Romance words (cf. ten Brink § 287). So we have English *un-* and Rom. *in-*; *mis-* and *mes-*; *a-* and *a-*; *in-* and *en-*. Usually the accentuation of Romance words with such prefixes corresponds with that of English words that are similarly compounded.

The occurrence in our texts of a considerable number of nouns with unaccented prefix, shows that the practice of accentuation varied, a state of matters which continued for a long time, partly even down to the present day.

In Chaucer we find the prefix more frequently unaccented than in the allit. poets, especially the prefixes *a, de,* but also others. This may be explained by his learned education, by his knowledge of French and Latin. Yet he also has occasionally the stress on the prefix. The uneducated among his contemporaries probably laid the stress more frequently on the prefix. The prevalence of stressed prefix in the allit. poets is due, partly to their smaller linguistic knowledge, partly to the requirements of the metre.

In early Mod. E., e. g. in Spenser, we not unfrequently find agreement of accentuation with Chaucer. So for example he stresses *entráile, trespás, (emprize), pourtráict,* &c. (cf. Koch's *Engl. Gr.*). Levins's accentuation agrees generally with that of the present day, but he has *contráct* and *desért.* On page 63 above we have exhibited examples from Boyer and Bailey of dissyllabic nouns with prefixes, in which the stress differs from that of the present day. These may be compared with the accentuations of Johnson (1755) in the same words: *accéss, assént, cómment, cóncert, cóncrete, contour* (marked as French), *cóntrast, cónsult* ("it is variously accented"), *device, devíse, discóunt, éngine, éxile* ("it seems anciently to have had the accent indifferently on either syllable: now it is uniformly on the first"), *íngress, ínvoice, perfúme, portént, precínct, preságe, preténce, próduce* ("This noun, though accented on the last syllable by *Dryden,* is generally accented on the former"), *próvost, recórd* ("the accent of the noun is indifferently on either syllable"), *survéy, cóntract* ("anciently accented on the first").

II. When we come, in the second place, to consider the accentuation of polysyllabic Nouns + Prefix, we shall find that some of the principles that determine the stress of dissyllables, operate also in the longer words. Here, as in dissyllabic words, the stress is more frequently laid on the prefix. So we have in *T. cónfusion, cóniuracioun, córupcioun, déleberacioun, délyuerans, déuocioun, díscrecioun,* &c. (v. p. 67 sq.); in *M. áuenture, cómmandement, cóndycyone,* &c. (v. p. 69); in *L. présumpcioun, répentance, cónstellacion,* &c. &c. (v. p. 69 sq.). In this respect, again, our alliterative poets closely agree among themselves, that is to say, Germanic or English accentuation prevails among them all.

1. Compounds with prefixes no longer felt as such, were treated like English words, and threw the stress back on the prefix, e. g. *émperour, óccidente.* This was necessarily the practice in syncopated forms like *áunter,* a contraction which points to an accentuation *áuenture.*

2. The stress of the noun is often influenced by that of the corresponding verb. Examples:

> *assémbly (T.* and *M.* always) *(assémblen),*
> *atténdant (atténden),*
> *encháuntement (encháunten),*
> *(dis)cóverour (discóveren),*
> *acórdaunce (accórden),*
> *conterróller (contrólen),*
> *absólucioun (absólven),*
> *allówance (allówen).*

Verbal nouns preserve the accent of their corresponding verbs: *indýting* like *indýten*; *despýsere* like *despýsen*.

The preceding verbs have all unstressed prefix, but frequently the latter bears the accent, as in *cómanden* in all our alliterative poets, while the syncopated form *cómse* points to an accentuation *cómmencen.*

Yet, in spite of the numerous cases in which the stress of noun and of corresponding verb agrees, there are many others in which such an agreement of accentuation is not found. So we have:

prócuratour, but *procúren,*
cónservatour, but *consérven,*
délyuerans, but *delívren,* yet, also *délivren,*
répentance, but *repénten,* yet, also *répentant,*
cómmandement, but *cománden,* yet, always *cómanden* in our allit.
  poets, but cf.

> *Ðe maundement of Moises þei marked to þat mayre*
>   *(Pist. of Swete Susan* v. 19),

púrveaunce, but *purvéyen,*
cónfessour, but *conféssen,*
présumption, but *presúmen,*
rémembrance, but *remémbren,*
prófessioun, but *proféssen,*
súggestion, but *suggésten,*
córrectour, but *corrécten,*
índulgence, but *indúlgen,*
óbservaunce, but *obsérven.*

In other cases, again, the stress conforms, not to that of corresponding verbs, but of other words derived from the same root. So:

> *déuocioun* with stress of *dévout,*
> *discrecioun* „ „ „ *díscret,*
> *cónfusioun* „ „ „ *cónfus,*
> *córupcioun* „ „ „ *córrupt.*

3. Sometimes the prefix appeared to be meaningless. Hence *supprioure* (like *príour*).

4. Here, as in dissyllabic nouns, we have compounds, the corresponding simple forms of which did either not exist, or had meanings unconnected with the compounds. Examples of such words are numerous: *déstenye, diskómfiture, cónsistorie, cóuenant* &c. &c.

5. In addition to the examples of unstressed prefix, enumerated under 2. p. 114, we have still other cases, like *avántage, affíaunce, apáreil,* &c., in which the prefix was still felt as such, and hence does not take the accent, which, according to the English principle, falls on the syllable following the prefix. In such cases Chaucer shows frequently a different accentuation. The various categories are here to be considered separately.

a) Words of 3 syllables like *emperour,* &c. Upon the whole, Chaucer's accentuation agrees with that of the allit. poets. French nouns, originally accented on the last syllable that is capable of receiving the stress, take in English the Germanic accent, while the original principal accent became secondary.

In Mod. E. there is in this respect a partial agreement with ME., but we also find the prefix unaccented, especially when corresponding verbs exist, as *repéntance, indúlgence, preférment,* &c. That this accentuation existed also partly in ME., is shown by the above mentioned exceptions *avántage, affíaunce, evidence,* &c., taken from the allit. poets.

Both ME. and Mod. E., therefore, show a diversity of practice in the accentuation or non-accentuation of prefixes, in cases where the value of these as such was still felt.

That in Chaucer we hardly find such prefixes unstressed, is partly owing to the scholarly feeling of the poet, who does not like entirely to neglect the French accentuation, or seeks at least to preserve it as a secondary stress. Hence, he accentuates *córrectòur, próvisòur, cónfessòur,* a pronunciation which was in close agreement with the popular one. But also the metre and the technical requirements of rhyme have exerted their influence. At the end of the verse, on account of the rhyme, an accentuation *próvisòur* is of course in its place, but in the middle of the verse, *provísour* would have produced a too heavy thesis and made the metre clumsy, as such words in ME. had still a secondary stress on the last accented syllable.

That this fluctuation in the stressing of such words continued in early Mod. E., may be seen from numerous examples in Shakspere (some of them adjectives): *cómmendàble* (cf. Oxf. Dict. s. v.), *confíscate, contráry, différent, obdúrate, oppórtune, prescíence, sepúlchre, siníster, cónfessor, córrosive, délectable, détestable, óbservant, énginer, píoner, plébeians, púrveyor, súccessor.* Nor are cases of this kind rare in English of the present day, and they may also be found in vulgar speech, e. g. *cónwayance, cóllection* (quoted from Dickens by Storm, *Engl. Philol.* p. 813).

The following are the examples from our texts, in which the prefix is stressed, and the accentuation of which agrees with Chaucer's. Those that are marked with an asterisk are not found in Chaucer, according to Skeat's glossary. Examples: *cóuenàunt, déstenỳ, óccidènt, cóuntenàunce, *cónysàunce, émperèsse, émperòur, *éuydènce, áventúre (aunter), púrveyànce, répentàunce, súccessòur, *cónfessòur, *rémembràunce, *córrectòur, índulgènce, *próvisòur, *préfermènt, résidúe* (O. Fr. *residu*).

Exceptions, in addition to those that have the accent of their corresponding verbs (v. p. 114), are the following: *avántage, affíaunce, apárail, arérage, eschéker, innócence, evídence.*

b) Words of **three** (or four) **syllables** like *remedie*, ending in *-ie*, are not numerous in the allit. poets, and have the stress on the prefix, except *injúrie*. Chaucer accents such words in two different ways: either *rémedỳ(e)*, or *remédie*, with Latin accentuation; so also *victórie* as well as *víctorìe*. The examples from our texts are: **cómissarie. (L), cónsistorie, cónstorie (L)* (Chaucer: *cónsistòrie*), *injúrie (M)* (Chaucer: *injúre, Troil.* III, 1018, O. Fr. *injure*), *cómpany.* In the accentuation of such words Mod. E., agrees with the allit. poets, i. e. the popular pronunciation has prevailed, as in *commissary, company,* but in others Mod. E. still shows variation of stress, as in *consistory.*

c) Words of more than three (four or five, seldom six) syllables and ending in *-ioun,* are usually stressed on the prefix, i. e. they have Germanic accentuation. Examples: *cóndiscoun* (*T. M.*), *cónfusion* (*T.*), *cóniuracioun* (*T.*), *córupcioun* (*T. L.*), *déleberacion* (*T.*), *déuocioun* (*T.*), *díscrecioun* (*T. L.*), *présumpcoun* (*T. L.*), *prócessione* (*M.*), *prótteccione* (*M.*), *cónstellacion* (*L.*), *cóntemplacion* (*L.*), *désperacion* (*L.*), *pérmutacion* (*L.*), *pérsecucion* (*L.*), *réstitucioun* (*L.*), *cóncepcion* (*L.*), *cóntricion* (*L.*), *prófession* (*L.*), *rélacion* (*L.*), *réligion* (*L.*), *rémission* (*L.*), *súggestion* (*L.*), *súspecion* (*L.*).

Exceptions: *compássion* (*T.*), *absólucion* (*L.* verb: *absólven*).

Chaucer's accentuation of such words diverges considerably from that of the allit. poets. He follows an accentuation based upon the Latin: *condícioun, devócioun, relígioun,* &c. (of four syllables).

còntempláciòun, dèsperáciòun, cònstelláciòun, &c. (of five syllables).

In those of six syllables, where the allit. poets have *déleberacioun,* Chaucer accentuates as in *albìficáciòun* (*Chan. Yem. T.* 805).

This Latin accentuation has gradually become universal in Mod. E. In early Mod. E. such words had still a secondary accent on the final syllable, as in the following examples from Gascoigne's *Steel Glas: conténtións* 823, *súperstítión* 866, *perféctiòn* 1048. Now only the principal accent on the syllable before the termination *-tion* is heard.

As in ME. such words had at least two accented syllables after the unaccented initial syllable (prefix), the introduction of the Germanic stress on the prefix would have produced an awkward series of unaccented syllables, or would perhaps have led to too great a mutilation of such words. Hence, they preserved the learned, Latin stress. (Cf. Gill in Ellis's *Early Engl. Pronunciation* III, p. 932). In the allit. poets the prevailing accentuation of the prefix in these words was probably partly adopted for the sake of the metre, or the rime-letter falls on an unaccented syllable, which constitutes a poetical licence. Yet this accentuation must have obtained in a certain measure, as is shown by early Mod. E. (Cf. the examples from Levins, quoted on pp. 70 and 71).

d) Other examples of compounds of more than three syllables, besides those ending in -*ioun* already mentioned, are not numerous in our texts. The allit. poets accentuate such words either on the prefix, or on the syllable next to it, especially when the force of the prefix was still felt. Examples with stress on prefix:

cónservatour (*T.*) (still so accented, or with stress on penultimate. Cf. Oxf. Dict. s. v.).
prócuratour (*L.*) (cf. *prócter*, and in Chaucer *prócutòur*).
cómandement (*T. M. L.* very often. In Chaucer *commándemènt*).
óbedyence (*L.* but Chaucer has *obédiènt*).
ádolescence (*L.*).
prósperitie (*L.* cf. the adj. *prospre* in Chaucer, but *prospéritèe*).

With stress next to prefix:
expériment (*T. L.*).
[*dis*]*skómfitoure* (*M.* often).
discomfáyture (*L.*, Chaucer: *discónfitùre*).
appúrtenaunce (*L.*, not in Chaucer's verse).
exécutour (*L.*, often, Chaucer: *exécutòur, exécutrìce*).
perséueraunce (*L.*, so in Chaucer; cf. the verb. *persévere*, which has this stress still in early Mod. E.).

Chaucer accents such words according to the requirements of the metre, with secondary stress on the final accented syllable, and chief stress two syllables further back.

Examples of these words occur only occasionally in *T.* and *M.*, and their accentuation is to be explained like that of words of more than three syllables without prefix. Most of the preceding examples are found in *L.*, but the stress on the prefix is not merely for the sake of the alliteration, as appears from *cómandement* (*com[m]ament* in *Curs. Mundì*), from Boyer's *cónservation, cónventicle, décampment*, from Bailey's *cónventicle, dísaster* (3 syll.), *inápplication, íncensory, ópponent* (3 syllables), *prógnosis* (3 syllables), and from accentuations like *áccessory, ádequacy, ádmirable, cómmonalty, déprecatory, éfficacy*, &c. Also accentuations in vulgar speech, like *cón-*

siderations, may here be referred to. (Cf. Storm, *Engl. Philol.* p. 813).

III. The accentuation of polysyllabic uncompounded nouns agrees generally with that of polysyllables with prefixes, the types being usually the same in both. These uncompounded nouns are of three, four, or five syllables, and are mostly of French origin. In French the accent lies either on the final syllable, or, when the word ends in unaccented *e*, on the penultimate, so that the French types are:

3 syllables	× × × ́	*garnison,*
	× × ́ ×	*arbitre,*
4 syllables	× × × × ́	*félicité,*
	× × × ́ ×	*sépulture,*
5 syllables	× × × × × ́	*satisfaction,*
	× × × × ́ ×	*évangéliste.*

The examples from our texts may therefore be classified as follows:

Nouns of three syllables:

French		ME.
× × × ́	*fféueryer(e)*	× ́ × × ́
„	*sácramen*	„
„	*áuditours*	
„	*díamownd*	
„	*gárnison*	
„	*pótestat*	
„	*béneson*	
„	*élement*	
„	*équite*	
„	*órisoun*	
„	*únite*	
„	*fórreours*	
„	*déuinour*	
„	*régratour*	
„	*cúratour*	
„	*méyntenour*	
„	*túrmentour*	„
„	*arbýtour*	× × ́ ×
× × ́ ×	*fénestres*	„ or × ́ × ×

French		ME.
× ×́ ×	*málese*	×́ × × or × ×́ ×
„	*méynprise*	„ „ „
„	*ensámple*	

maríners (*M.*) but *márynerse* (*T.*).

Hence, in most of the examples of trisyllables, secondary stress was laid on the syllable accented in French, and the chief stress was placed on the first syllable. This is also Chaucer's accentuation, and, generally, what we find in Mod. E.

Nouns of four syllables:

French		ME.
× × × ×́	*avísement*	×́ × × ×̀
„	*embúschement*	„
„	*ábilíte*	×́ × × ×̀ or × ×́ × ×̀
„	*líyuyatan*	„ „ „
„	*nóbil(i)te*	„ „ „
„	*páuilyon*	„ „ „
„	*sólemnity*	„ „ „
„	*léuetenaunt*	
„	*póssession*	„ „ „
„	*dámpnacioun*	„ „ „
„	*sólstacion*	„ „ „
„	*díuinite*	„ „ „
„	*félicite*	„ „ „
„	*fráternite*	„ „ „
„	*fýsician*	„ „ „
„	*grámarien*	„ „ „
„	*sáluacion*	„ „ „
„	*vírginite*	„ „ „
× × ×́ ×	*fántasye*	×́ × ×̀ ×
„	*cóuytise*	„
„	*spécerye*	
„	*rétenaunce*	
„	*álmaries*	
„	*órdinaunce*	
„	*tábernacle*	
„	*cón(e)stable*	
„	*sépulture*	
„	*avánttwarde*	„ or × ×́ × ×

French		ME.
× × ×́ ×	*avéntaile*	× ×́ × × or ×́ × × ×̀
„	*aváwmbrace*	„ „ „
„	*áudience*	
„	*bénefice*	
„	*rétenaunce*	
„	*máyntenaunce*	„
„	*fílosofer*	×́ × ×̀ × (or × ×́ × ×̀).

We have here two kinds of types. The first: × × × ×́ of the French, leads to the type ×́ × × ×̀ in the allit. poets, to × ×́ × ×̀ in Chaucer. The former draw back the accent as far as possible from the end, usually on the radical syllable, being the Germanic accent, the latter accentuates according to the principles of Latin pronunciation (cf. *supra*), and according to the metre. In Mod. E. the stress in these words (in so far as they are not obsolete), agrees with that of Chaucer, but some of them have been shortened into trisyllables, like *salvation, physician,* &c. Of the second type, × × ×́ × of the French, producing in the allit. poets and in Chaucer the type ×́ × ×̀ ×, we also have a considerable number of examples. All of them (when not obsolete), except *fílosofer*, have the same stress in Mod. E. and (except *tabernacle*) become trisyllables.

Nouns of five syllables:

French		ME.
× × × × ×́	*satisfáccion*	⎰ ×̀ × × ×́ × ×
	sátisfaccion	⎱ ×́ × × ×̀ × ×
	géneracioun	„
	mítigacioun	
„	*lámentacioun*	„
× × × ×́ ×	*ýmag(e)ry(e)*	⎰ ×́ × × × ×̀ ×
„	*déseueraunce*	⎱ × ×́ × × ×̀ × (Ch.)
	téologye	„
	ýpocrisie	
	álconomye	„
	ástronomy(e)	×́ × × ×̀ (×)
	(astromye	×́ × × ×̀ × Ch.)
	euángelist(e)	× ×́ × ×̀ (×)

Here the allit. poets mostly accentuate on the first syllable. Chaucer usually agrees with Mod. E. except in *ymag(e)ry(e)*. The modern accentuation of the latter agrees with that of our poets, and the word consists of three syllables, in Chaucer of four. The other words have now four syllables, with stress, in four cases, on the third, in five others, on the second syllable.

Chaucer has *másoneries* (*H. of F.* 1303), *ýmageries* (Skeat's accentuation, *ymagéries,* in the Glossary, cannot be adopted).

IV. **Dissyllabic Nouns (including trisyllables with final unaccented *e*) without Prefix** have in our texts the stress on the first syllable, except *uságe,* and the obsolete *orfráy(e).* These two have preserved the French accentuation. In the *Rom. of the Rose* we find *órfrays* (cf. p. 76 above). Chaucer frequently preserves the original stress in such words: *pitée, honóur,* &c., but often also *pítee, hónour,* &c. (cf. ten Brink, § 284). In earlier ME. we also find this diversity of accentuation. In *King Horn: burdón, folýè, homágè, manérè,* &c. but also *géaunt, cástel,* &c. (cf. Wissmann *QF.* 16, p. 47).[1] *cúmbranse* has the stress of the verb *cúmbren, spélonkes,* Lat. *spelunca,* has here the Germanic accent, the classical accentuation was probably also in use (cf. p. 76 above).

That the French accentuation was preserved, was no doubt owing mostly to the requirements of the rhyme, rather than to the influence of Continental or Anglo-Norman French. This influence of rhyme is still seen even in early Mod. E., especially in Spenser, whose language, however, is sometimes artificially archaic. He has, for example, the rhyme *horrór : yore.* (Cf. Koch, *Engl. Gram.*) Words of later introduction, i. e. after the ME. period, present the same fluctuation of accent. So we find in Levins: *parént, cément.* In Boyer: *càmpain, cément, crávat, mánure, placárd, trefóil, triphthóng.* In Bailey: *bázar, cadénce, chémise, devóir* (already ME.), *dívan, fermént, mirró(u)r* (perhaps a misprint; the word is already ME.), (*prismóid*), *rómance,* (already ME.), *sapphíre* (already ME.), (*spheróid*), *turmóil.* In Johnson: *devóir, placárd* (*prismóid*), (*sphéroid*), *cément.*

---

[1] Cf. also Pabst, *Robert of Gloucester,* Berlin Diss. 1889, p. 13, and Kunze, *Bodi and Soule,* Berlin Diss. 1892, p. 39, where examples are given of the two accentuations: *tresóur, resóun; glótoun, pálays.*

Adjectives and Adverbs.

In these the principles of accentuation agree generally with those that we have indicated for Nouns. In a few cases the stress conforms to that of corresponding Verbs. It will, therefore, suffice to classify them.

I. Dissyllabic Adjectives with prefix. Most of them have the prefix stressed: *díscrete* (*T.*), *cónfus* (*L.*), *présent* (*L.*), *díyuers* (*M.*), *sékere* (*M.*), *íngrat* (*L.*). With unaccented prefix: *distráct* (*T.*), *appérte* (*M.*).

These accentuations are often at variance with the modern stress. But such deviations occur also in the lexicographers of the 18th century, and not only in such words as are found already in ME., but also in others that were introduced in Mod. E. times, and in which the preservation of the French-Latin stress can cause no surprise. So, in Boyer we find: *compléx, concréte, cónform, profóund*. In Bailey: *compóund, cónform, contríte, ingráte, refléx, transvérse*. In Johnson: *contríte, ingráte, refléx, transvérse*.

Dissyllabic Adjectives without prefix all have the stress on the first syllable: *bénygn(e)* (*L.*), *déuyne* (*T.*), *érraunt* (*L.*), *géntille* (*M.*), *áusterne* (*T.*). Differences from modern usage are again seen in Boyer: *áugust, gallánt, máture*. In Bailey: *áugust, jéjune, jucúnd, mundáne, servíle*. In Johnson: *fecúnd, jocúnd, mundáne*.

II. Trisyllabic Adjectives with prefix also mostly stress the latter: *áuenaunt* (*T., M.*), *déuowtlich(e)* (*L.*), *díssyrus* (*T.*), *éxcellent* (*T.*), *ápparant* (*M.*), *récreaunt* (*M., L.*). With unaccented prefix: *dispítus* (*T.*), *enuýous* (*M.*), *impárfit* (*L.*), *impácient* (*L.*), *innócent* (*L.*).

III. Those without prefix are accented on the first syllable: *órrible* (*M.*), *áusterene* (*M.*), *cóntrary* (*T.*), *méruailous* (*M.*), *rébawdous* (*M.*), *sémblable* (*L.*), *sólempne* (*T., M.*), but *amírous* (*L.*).

Deviations from modern usage in Boyer are, with prefix: *cómplaisant, cónsummate, córrosive, desperáte, indúrate, protéstant, recondìte, redólent, retrogràde, subaltérn*. Without prefix: *alternàte, fállacious, ràpacious, ridicúle* (cf. p. 83 above). Bailey has with prefix: *complaisánt, concussíve, confíscate, emánent, imbécile, infámous, mischíevous, recóndite, subaltérn(s)*.

Without prefix: *avárous, cavérnous, cháotic, contráry, jovíal, juveníle, labórant, matrónal, patrónal, phlégmatick, satúrnine, schísmatick, tempestíve, tripartíte.* Some of those accentuations are confirmed by Johnson: with prefix he has: *complaisánt, confíscate, corrósive,* ("It was anciently pronounced with the accent on the first syllable") *imbécile, recóndite, súbaltern.* Without prefix: *labórant, patrónal, rhéumatick, splénetick, schísmatick, stígmatick.*

IV. Polysyllabic Adjectives have, with only three exceptions, the stress on the first syllable: *cóuenable (T.), présumptius (T.), rélygeous (M., L.), córageous (M.), cómpanable (L.), dílitable (L.), óffíciales (L), próffitable (T., M., L.), cóllateral (L.), párauenture (L), próuincials (L.), órientales (L.), ýmaginatif (L.).* The exceptions are: *depártable, immésurables, impóssible,* all from Langland.

For the examples from Levins, Boyer, and Bailey, in which the accentuation differs from the present one, the reader is referred to pp. 83 and 84 above. We shall only add those from Johnson, which mostly confirm the accentuation given by his contemporaries: *desúltory, ammoníac* (cf. Bailey p. 83), *empyréan, exémplary, falsifíable, remédiless* (so also the noun and the verb *remédy*).

V. Adverbs. These are few in number, and, except *cúrtesly (T.),* are all compounds without the stress on the prefix or preposition: *apás (M.), avíssely (M.), affórse (L.), apárte (L.), arére (L.).*

Verbs.

For the purpose of examining the accentuation of verbs in our texts, we may classify them according to their formation, i. e. we may separate those with prefixes from those without prefixes.

a) Verbs with prefixes.

The· practice of accentuation shows considerable divergency, according to the nature of the prefix, and we, therefore, arrange the compound verbs here by their various prefixes. *a (ab, ad, ex).*

With only two exceptions, *ássembled (T.)* and *áunter (T., M., L.),* the former doubtful (cf. p. 102), all verbs with this prefix leave the latter unstressed. This agrees generally with the usage in Mod. E., in which also this prefix is rarely stressed, as in *ádvertise* (but cf. Oxf. Dict. s. v.; Johnson has *advertíse*), *ággregate*, *ággravate*, *állocate*, *áspirate*. In Levins we find, however, *ábsent*, *áccent*, both, no doubt, influenced by the corresponding adjective and noun. Boyer accents: *àpply*, *át-tract*; Bailey: *ábsent*, *árray*.

com (*con, col, cor*) stressed:

cómford (*T.*), *cómpast* (*T.*), *cónquerid* (*M.*), *cómaund* (*T., M., L.*), *cómende* (*T., L.*), *cómyn* (*T.* i. e. *commune*), *cómpilet* (*T.*), *cónfermyt* (*T., L.*), *cónsumet* (*T.*), *cónfusede* (*M.*), *cónuaye* (*M.*), *cóniured* (*L.*), *cónsenteth* (*L.*), *cónspire* (*L.*), *cónstreyne* (*L.*), *cónstrue* (*L.*), *cóntreue* (*L.*), *cónuerted* (*L.*), *córrette* (*L.*), *cónnse* (*T., L.*), *cóngeyde* (*L.*), *cónsider* (*T.*), *cóntynu* (*T., L.*).

com &c. unstressed:

confóundit (*T.* but also *cónfound, T., M., L.*), *consáyuit* (*T.*, but also *cónsayuit, T., L.*), *confórmen* (*L.*, but also *cónfourmen, L.*), *counsáyles* (*M.*, but also *cóunseile, T., M., L.*).

The prefix *com* also appears stressed in the majority of cases, while the verbs in which this prefix remains unaccented, all occur likewise, and most of them more frequently, with the prefix stressed.

In Mod. E. too, the accentuation varies, sometimes even in the same word, as in *compensate, constellate*, in both of which Johnson accents the verbal part. In Levins we find *cómprehend*; Boyer has: *cóllate, cónjoin, cónsent, cóntract*.

conter, counter stressed:

The examples are few, only *cónterfeteth* (*L.*), *cóntreplede* (*L.*), and *cóuntersegge* (*L.*).

The first of these is still so accented, perhaps the only example in Mod. E. *countersign* is pronounced with level stress, or at least with only secondary stress on the prefix. Boyer marks *cóuntermand*.

de stressed:

désteynid (*T.*), *déuydyt* (*T., L.*), *déuysede* (*T., M., L.*), *désyred* (*T.*), *díscendis* (*M.*), *dístitur* (*T.*), *déuorande* (*M.*), *dépose* (*L.*), *déspeir* (*L.*).

de unstressed:

deménez (*T., M.*), *denýet* (*T.*), *defámed* (*L.*), *defýed* (*L.*), *depráue (L.), detérmynet (T. L.), defádide (M.), defóulede (T., L.), discréue (L.).*

de stressed or unstressed:

déclaret (T.), decláret (T., L.); déliuer (T., M., L.), delýuered (L.); délited (T., L.), delíted (T.); déssauis (= deceive, T., L.), dissáiue (T.); dísseruet (= deserve, T., L.), disséruyt (T., L.); défende (L.), deféende (L.); départen (L.), depértid (T., L.); désstroye (L.), distróy (T.); díspise (L.), dispíset (T., L.).

The prefix *de* appears to be nearly as frequently stressed as unstressed, while in the case of the verbs that show this prefix sometimes with the accent and sometimes without, the practice is also pretty evenly balanced. Levins has *déstil*; Boyer *décamp, déter,* in which the verbal part is now accented.

dis stressed:

dísputyng (L.), dísplese (L.), désauowe (L.), dísalowed (L.), disconfit (L.), dísassent (T.).

dis unstressed:

distrácte (T.), díschárgen (L.), deráyne (T.; cf. Oxf. Dict. s. v.).

Here again the practice of stressing the prefix preponderates. Levins still has *díscontinew.* Now the prefix *dis* is rarely accented in verbs: *díscipline* and *dístance* have the stress of the nouns from which they are derived; *díslocate* is accented like the older (cf. Oxf. Dict.) participial adjective. The accentuation of *díssipate* may perhaps be explained in a similar manner; the verb is at least also made from the (Latin) participial form.

en, in.

This prefix occurs stressed only in *éntyce,* in *L.,* doubtfully in *M.* (cf. p. 93); *encombre* has the prefix stressed as well as unstressed in *L.; endited,* stressed and unstressed in *L.,* but only unaccented in *M.* All the other verbs, a considerable number, in our texts, leave this prefix unstressed. In Mod. E. *en* is always unaccented in verbs, *in* not unfrequently accented, as in most trisyllabic verbs ending in *-ate,* and derived, like *díslocate,* mentioned above, from Latin participial forms. Such verbs are: *íllustrate* (also *illústrate*), *ímitate, ímmigrate, ímmolate, ímplicate,* &c. But also *incúlcate, inspíssate,* learned words of comparatively modern formation.

e, es, ex stressed:
>*éxcepte (L.), éxcused (L.).*

e, es, ex unstressed:
>*exchéwe (T., M.), excúsit (T.), eschápe (M.), ascápie (L.), escháunges (L.), expóunen (L.).*

The examples with accented prefix occur only in *L.*

In Mod. E. the prefix is accented only in such verbs as *éducate, élevate, émanate, énervate* (cf. Oxf. Dict. s. v.), *éxcavate, éxculpate* (but also *excúlpate*, cf. Oxf. Diet. s. v.) &c. (cf. the remark above under *en, in*). Boyer accents: *éradicate*; Bailey: *emígrate, excávate.*

enter (inter) occurs only stressed:
>*énteres (T.), éntermeten (L.).* In Mod. E. we have *ínterest, ínterview*, both with the accent of their respective nouns; *intérpolate* and *intérrogate* have the stress on the antepenult like others in *-ate* of four or more syllables. Levins has *énterlace.*

ob (oc, of, op) stressed:
>*ócupyes (T., M., L.).*

ob (oc, of, op) unstressed:
>*obéy (T.), offéndit (T.), opprésse (T.).*

The accentuation here agrees with that in Mod. E., in which, besides *occupy*, only *óffer* has the stress on the prefix. The latter existed already in OE. as *offrian*, and had acquired the Germanic accentuation.

per occurs only stressed:
>*pérsauit (T., M., L.), péruersede (M.), párforme (L.), pérmute.*

pre also occurs only stressed:
>*présent (T., M., L.), présumed (L.).*

pro likewise is stressed in all the examples:
>*prófers (M.), prócure (T.), púrsue (T., L.), púruay (T., M., L.), prófesside (M.), púrtrayede (M.), prónouncid (L.).*

Boyer has: *pórtray, prólong, prógnosticate.*

In Mod. E. the last three prefixes are more frequently unaccented, though examples of verbs in which they are stressed are not rare, as *pércolate, prédicate, prócreate*, &c. It forms no part of the present treatise to present a complete list of such verbs.

re stressed:

> *réscow* (*T.*, *M.*), *ráunsound* (*M.*), *réceyuit* (*T.*, *M.*, *L.*), *rélesh* (*T.*), *rémeve* (*T.*, *M.*, *L.*), *rétaynit* (*T.*), *réwardet* (*T.*, *L.*), *rébuke* (*M.*, *L.*), *répent* (*M.*, *L.*), *réquit* (*M.*), *réstreynede* (*M.*), *rétournes* (*M.*), *réuenge* (*M.*), *réuerssede* (*M.*), *réuertede* (*M.*), *récorded* (*L.*), *réfuse* (*L.*), *réioyse* (*L.*), *réleue* (*L.*), *réffourmed* (*L.*), *réuerenced* (*L.*), *rémembirde* (*M.*), *récomendeth* (*L.*), *réconfordet* (*L.*), *réhetede* (*M.*), *rélayes* (*M.*), *répendez* (*M.*), *réueste* (*M.*, *L.*), *réclused* (*L.*), *récrayed* (*L.*), *réneye* (*L.*).

re unstressed:

> *resórt* (*T.*), *recláyme* (*L.*), *relýed* (*L.*, v. p. 97), *rekéuered* (*L.*), *recóunseld* (*T.*, v. p. 102), *repúgnet* (*T.*, *L.*).

re stressed or unstressed:

> *réstore* (*T.*), *restóre* (*T.*); *réherse* (*M.*, *L.*), *rehérse* (*L.*); *répreue* (*L.*), *repréued* (*T.*).

Of verbs compounded with *re*, the cases in which it is accented are greatly in excess of those in which it is unstressed. It is the reverse in Mod. E., in which verbs with accented *re* are rare, mostly cases in which the prefix is not readily recognised, such as *ránsom*, *rélish*, *réscue*, *rénder*, besides in *réconcile* and *récognise*. Levins has also *récommend* and *réprehend*.

Verbs compounded with *sub* and *super* are not numerous in our texts. In all the examples these prefixes are stressed. *Trans* occurs stressed in *tréspassed* (*L.*), unstressed in *transláted* (*T.*).

The preceding arrangement of the compounded verbs of Romance origin, suggests a few observations, which we now proceed to offer.

The prefixes beginning with vowels are mostly unstressed, which may, to a small extent, be due to the fact that vowel alliteration is comparatively rare. The verbs in which such prefixes are stressed, occur nearly all in *L*, whose alliteration, as we have had frequently occasion to remark, is not always to be trusted, and often does not agree with the true accentuation. But that these prefixes were sometimes really stressed in the spoken language, is proved by such words as *áunter*, *óccupy*, in which the prefix was no longer recognised, so that these words acquired the Germanic accentuation. As long, however, as these prefixes were still felt as such, the verbs compounded with them were treated like those of Germanic derivation with inseparable prefix, i. e. the verbal part was stressed.

But also in the case of those prefixes that begin with consonants, the question whether the particles still made their original force felt or not, is an important consideration in explaining the practice of accentuation in such compounds. Where the force of the prefix was not understood, the latter took the accent, for which we have direct proof in those verbs in which the prefix became so closely incorporated with the verb as to be entirely obscured, e. g. in *comse, cómaund, cónster, prófer, próker, réscow, ráunsound, sóiorne*, &c.

The fact that in a considerable number of compound verbs in our texts, the prefix is sometimes stressed, sometimes unstressed in the same word, shows that usage, in point of accentuation, was still to a considerable extent unsettled.

That the practice of drawing the accent back on the first syllable of the compound, was not carried even further than it shows itself in our examples, is no doubt, to some extent, due to a lingering knowledge of the origin of such words, to an acquaintance with French or Latin, from which these words were derived.

In verbs in which the prefix was apparently meaningless, it could be dropped, as in *(de)struien, (di)spense, (de)sputen, de(fenden), (di)skomfyted, di(sport)* (cf. Behrens, *Beiträge,* p. 64, sq. and Skeat, *Principles* II, chapter V).

Lastly, in some cases, in which the prefix is stressed, partly in opposition to modern accentuation, we may perhaps trace the influence of corresponding nouns or adjectives, as in *cómford, cómpast, córrette, déspeir, présent, réuenge.*

The learned Chaucer usually accents the radical part of the verb, both in compounds and in uncompounded verbs.

For the rules that guide his accentuation, with the exceptions, we may refer the reader to ten Brink, l. c. §§ 289 to 292.

b) Verbs without prefixes.

These are few in number in our texts, and nearly all of them have the accent on the first syllable. Each verb may, however, be considered by itself.

fórraye (*M.*), from OF. *forrer*, with stress on the final syllable, would naturally, in English, draw back the accent to the first syllable.

méruailles (*M.*) has the accent of its noun, in OF. *merveille*, with stress on the second syllable. Both the E. and the F. accentuations of the word existed in ME.; the former is proved, not only by the alliteration in *M*, but also by the forms *mervel*, *merval* (cf. Behrens p. 146).

cóueite (*L.*), from OF. *coveitier*, has preserved the radical stress of the original Latin, or rather, French unaccented *u* has received the stress in English (cf. Behrens pp. 116, 138).

órdainet (*T.*, *M.*, *L.* nine times). The same accentuation occurs also in *Curs. Mund.* (Morris and Skeat *Spec.* VII, 31). On the other hand, Behrens (p. 140) quotes examples in which the rhyme shows that also the second syllable was stressed, as in Mod. E. Both accentuations, therefore, obtained in ME.

sálute (*T.*), *sáluzed* (*M.*), F. *saluer*, shows the stress of the noun *sálus*, OF. *salut*. Chaucer has *saléwe* (v. p. 100 above).

tóurmentez (*M.*) has the stress of the noun, by which that of the verb was no doubt influenced.

cómbir (*T.*), OF. *combrer*, a dissyllabic verb, has of course the stress on the first syllable.

córonyd (*T.*). The syncopated form *crunen* and the form *coroune* show that the verb had the stress also on the second syllable. This accentuation is the original one, and existed by the side of that found in *T*. We may also compare the modern *córoner* and the dialectic or popular *crowner*. (Cf. Oxf. Dict. *crowner*).

The following verbs are compounds, although without prefixes:

édifyen (*L.*), originally *èdifíen* (F. *édifier*, ten Brink § 290), became *édifìen* by interchange of chief and secondary accent.

meyntène (*L.*), *máintene* (*T.*, *M.*, *L.*). The form *mainteynen*, which also occurs in ME., and the modern *maintain*, show that the verb was accented on the second syllable, but *máintene,* with the accent thrown back on the first syllable, must also have been heard. We have recorded sixteen examples of the verb with this accentuation from all the text.

méynprise (L.). The accentuation of the noun varies (cf. p. 76). The word is rare also as verb, and we cannot determine the accentuation with any certainty. Modern dictionaries, such as *The Encyclopædic* and *The Century,* place the accent on the first syllable of both noun and verb.

Chapter III.

C. Proper Names.

In dealing with the accentuation of foreign Proper Names, we should premise that our alliterative poets show considerable carelessness in the treatment both of the form and of the stress of such names. With the imperfect culture of those poets, the correct accentuation was either unknown to them, or they stressed their proper names according to the exigencies of the alliteration. Hence, the same proper names frequently occur with a different stress. Of the greater part of such foreign names our poets derived their knowledge only from written works, so that their accentuation is not regulated by the real and correct pronunciation, but is often entirely arbitrary. To this must be added that the proper names appear occasionally in quite mutilated forms, or even owe their origin to the imagination of the poets themselves, or to the romantic models from which they worked. Chaucer also frequently accentuates his proper names according to the requirements of the metre, and in his works too the stress often varies. (Cf. ten Brink, § 294).

We adopt the following classification of the proper names in our texts: 1. Dissyllabic Proper Names (including those with final unaccented e), a) with stress on the first syllable, b) with stress on the second syllable. 2. Proper Names of three syllables, a) with stress on the first syllable, b) with stress on the second syllable. 3. Proper Names of four or more syllables, a) with stress on the first syllable, b) with stress on the second syllable, c) with stress on the third syllable.

1a. Dissyllabic Proper Names with stress on the first syllable.

a) in the *Troy-Book*:

Cáster, Cástor, 1014, 1149.

Cólchos, 152.

Dáres, 60.

Dýtes, 60 (= *Dictys*).

Gádes, 311.

Gýdo, 54.

Hómer, 38.

Ítaile, 12906.

Jáson, 128, 131, 196, 210, 249, 286, &c.

Láerte, Láertus, 13661, 13663.

Néptune, 1536, 6094.

Néstor, 1147, 1190, 1226, 1257, 2035, 3565, 3572.

Óvid, 123.

Páyone, Páyuon, 2569, 5472 (= *Pœonia*).

Phílmene, 5493 (= *Pylœmenes*).

Páris, Párys, 2388, 2468, 2508, 2599.

Phílon, 1036, 1946 (= *Pylos*).

Póllux, 1015, 1150, 1215.

Sálerne, 6347 (= *Salernum*).

Thétas, 1558. (In Guido *Chetas*).

Vírgill, 1493.

Vólcaun, 4383.

Xánthus, 1602.

Árgon, 287.

Áscane, 6108 (= *Ascanius*).

Átthenes, 67.

Éctor, 1707, 2161.

Éson, 115.

b) in the *Morte Arthure*:

Báldake, 586 (= *Bagdad*, according to Brock).

Básille, 907.

Báyone, 38, 2379.

Báyous, 587.

Bédvere, Bédwere, 893, 1170, 1264, 1606, 2238, 2379.

Bédwar, 2384. (Cf. Branscheid, p. 197).

Bédwyne, 1408. (Cf. Br. p. 192).

Bélyne, 277. (In Malory *Bellinus*).

Bérade, 2384.

Bérelle, Bérille, Bérylle, 1264, 1433, 1605, 1771, 1775, 1914. (In Malory *Ber(i)el*).

Bérnarde, 566.

Brémyne, 277. (Cf. Br. pp. 183, 277).

Búrdeux, 38.

Brýane, 1606.

Búrgoyne, 36, 1018, 1241, 2383, like modern *Búrgundy*.

Cádor, Cádore, Cádors, Cádour, 247, 259, 481, 1602, 1637, 1707, 1718, 1724, 1777, 4188.

Cátrike, 482.

Cáyous, Káyous, 156, 209, 892, 1152, 1194, 1864, 1997, 2157. (Cf. Br. p. 191).

Chártris, 1619 (= *Chartres*).

Chéldrike, 2954.

Clárent, Clárente, 4193, 4202.

Clégis, Clégys, 1604, 1628, 1649, 1671, 1692, 1828, 1865, 2497, 3635, 4265. (Cf. Br. p. 194).

Clówdmur, 1604.

Cóllbrande, 2123, 2201. (Cf. Br. p. 196).

Cólome, 623.

Córnett, Córnette, 600, 1909 (= *Corneto*, according to Brock).

Cráddoke, Crádoke, 3487, 3511, 3517. (In Malory *Cradok*).

Dámaske, 578.

Flórent, fflórent, Flórente, 2255, 2483, 2729, 2735, 2762, 2764, 2797, 2803, 3018, 3112.

Gáluth, Gáluthe, 1387, 1470, 2558, 3709.

Gáwayne, Gáwaynne, Gáweayne, 1265, 1352, 1368, 1468, 2218, 3860.

Gáynour, 84, 705.

Gérarde, 2896.

Gérnaide, 2943.

Gérone, 863.

Géryne, 3708.

Gódarde, Góddarde, 496, 562, 2655, 3104.

Gódfraye, 3430.

Hárdelfe, Hárdolfe, 1741, 2974, 3583.

Víterbe, 326, 353, 2025, 2048, 3164.

Výenne, 41 (= *Vienne*, according to Brock).

Wálchere, 2680. (Cf. Br. p. 214.)

Wáynore, Wáynour, 233, 652, 657, 697, 3550, 3575. (Cf. *Gáynour*, p. 114 above).

Wécharde, 2495. (Cf. Br. p. 213.)

Whýcher, Wýchere, 2678, 2680, 4025. (Cf. Br. p. 214).

Áffrike, Áffryke, Áufrike, Áwfrike, 574, 1869, 2607, 3933.

Ákyne, 496 (= *Aachen*. Cf. Brock, Index).

Álgere, 2837.

Álmaygne, Álmayne, 45, 496, 555, 618, 2387, 3210, 3596.

Ántele, 2829.

Arthur(e), 288, 470, 496, 508, 519, 618, 625. (Cf. Br. p. 221).

Asye, 574.

Awguste, 1967.

Éctor, 2603, 2635.

Égipt, 576, 2200.

Érrake, 4075, 4161, 4263.

Éruge, 42.

Éstriche, 45, 3933 (= *Oesterreich*; cf. Brock).

Éwane, Éwayne, 337, 2066, 3973, 4075, 4161, 4263. (Cf. Malory, Sommer's List of Names: *Vwayne*).

Íoncke, 1739, 1868; *Ionéke*, 1905.

Órcage, 572.

Órigge, 1825.

Vnwyne, 2868.

c) in *Piers the Plowman*:

Bérnard, Bérnarde, B 4, 121; A 11, 41; B 15, 59, 414.

Félice, Félyce, A 5, 29; B 12, 47 (= *Felicia*, according to Skeat).

Fráunceys, B 15, 226.

Gálys, A 4, 110 (= *Gallicia*, according to Skeat).

Gódfrei, A 5, 167.

Láurence, Láurens, C 3, 130; C 18, 64.

Máhon, Máhoun, B 13, 82; C 19, 151; C 21, 295. (This stress also in Chaucer).

Mérgrete, A 4, 37.

Pérnel, Péronelle, Púrnele, A 4, 102; A 5, 26, 45, 163; B 5, 26, 160; C 18, 71 (= Lat. *Petronilla*. Cf. Skeat).

Ráchel, A Pr. 108.

Sáturne, A 7, 311.

Abel, C 19, 231, 319.

Ádam, A 1, 63; A 6, 93; A 11, 275; B 11, 200, 407; C 11, 213;
    B 12, 233; B 16, 81, 205; B 18, 143, 176, 193, 278, 356; B 19,
    54; C 19, 68, 231; C 21, 157.

Ágag, A 3, 247, 266.

Ámbrose, B 13, 38; B 19, 264.

Éleyne, B 5, 110.

Ýsay, Ýsaye, A 11, 275; B 16, 81 (= *Isaiah*).

d) in Richard the Redeles:

Félice, 3, 160.

Pérnell, 3, 156.

1b. Dissyllabic Proper Names with stress on the second syllable.

In the Morte Arthure:

Gawáyne, Gawáynne, 233, 2979.   (Cf. p. 134 above).

Ionéke, 1905.   (Cf. p. 136 above).

With only two exceptions, the dissyllabic proper names have the accent on the first syllable, and these exceptions occur also with stress on the first syllable. Many of these names preserve the classical form and accent, such as *Cástor, Dáres, Póllux*, &c. Others, like *Hómer, Néptune, Vírgil*, &c., have adopted a shortened form, perhaps through the French, and have drawn back their accent to the first syllable. In Chaucer such names are often accented cn the final syllable. The accent is also drawn back in most of the names (nearly all non-classical) in the *Morte Arthure*.

2a. Proper Names of three syllables with stress on the first syllable.

a) in the Troy-Book:

Áchilles, 2729, 2741, 7441, 7636.

Ámysones, 5522.

Áries, 1053.

Áschatus, 13637 (= *Acastus*).

Amphimak, Ámphimake, Amphimakus, 4081, 4114, 7682, 11378.

Apolyn, Appolyne, áppollyne, 4263, 4280, 4387, 8133, 8734, 11954, 11962.

Bóetes, 5485.

Cápadoys, 7496.

Cápidus, 5453.

Cássandra, Cássandray, 1496, 3467, 7175, 11808.

Clúnestra, 12714, 12721, 12729, 12733, 12745.

Cólophon, 5439. (In Guido *Colofon*).

Cúpenor (?), 6384. (In Guido *Capenor*).

Déffebus, 2449, 2476, 2492, 2494, 2797, 6011 (= *Deiphobus*).

Díana, 4659.

Díomed, Dýamede, 3653, 4946.

Dónori, 4082 (= *Diores*).

Dýnadron, 6764. (In Guido *Dinadaron*).

Écuba, 1471, 2505, 2694.

Élenus, Élinus, 2478, 2540, 2713, 3907.

Éneas, 1491, 2799, 5096, 6216, 6855.

Ércules, 288, 294, 819, 1021, 1871, 5192.

Éripa, 6617 (= *Hiripisus*).

Gálathe, 6245.

Hélminus, 4068 (= *Ialmenus*).

Hýlias, 1559. (In Guido *Heleas*).

Iácomas, 6834. (In Guido *Ieconias*).

Ióbiter, 291 (= *Jupiter*).

Lámydon, 1001. 1209, 1221, 1229, 1284, 1300, 1391, 1417, &c.

Lúcifer, 4417.

Lýcomede, 13393, 13435.

Mánsua, 1788 (= *Magnesia*).

Mássidon, 313.

Médea, 124, 391, 431, 595, 609, 669, 690, 856, 973, 986, 989.

Mélapsa, 13471.

Mínerva, Mýner[v]a, 4380, 12541.

Módernus, 6793.

Páfflegon, 5489.

Pálades, Pýlades, 2384, 2410.

Pátroclus, 3652, 6313.

Pélleus, 113, 142, 195, 247, 1033, 1043, 1092, 1161, 1787.

Péndragon, 5436.

Póterhas, 4098 (= *Podarces*).

Prócholus, 6382. (In Guido *Prochailus*).
Prótheno, Prótheus, 2667, 2715, 4063.
Próthenor, 6336 (= *Prothoenor*).
Próthylus, 4121.
Sálame, 1828 (= *Salamis*).
Ségurda, 6337.
Sélidus, 6343 (= *Schedius*).
Séripes, 6181.
Sérpidon, 5448.
Síthera, Sítheria, Sýtheria, 2842, 2973, 2989 (= *Cythera*).
Stígeta, 13169. (In Guido *Strigonas*).
Sýmagon, 5509. (In Guido *Sigamon*).
Sýnabor, 6087. (In Guido *Cincinabor*).
Sýtrinos, 2845. (In Guido *Citrius*).
Télamon, and the derivative form *Télamonius* (= *Ajax*), 1027,
    1131, 1160, 1829, 2033, 7083.
Ténydon, 3268 (= *Tenedos*).
Thélephus, 4106, 1591. (In Guido *Telepalus*).
Thóantes, 11738.
Trícerda, 1558. (In Guido *Timbrea*).
Trísion, 4102. (In Guido *De regno tricionico*).
Tróiana, 1558.
Tróilus, Tróylus, 1487, 2553.
V́lexes, V́lixes, 4945, 13117.
Xántipus, 6107.
Ýmasus, 5445. (In Guido *Imasius*).

b) in the *Morte-Arthure*:

Ábsolone, 2868.
Áladuke, Ályduke, 1739, 1824. (Cf. Br. p. 194, and Sommer in
    Malory).
Álymere, 4078.
Árraby, 576.
Ámyone, 42 (= *Aniane*, according to Brock).
Áschinour, 1824.
Áueloyne, 4309.
Báwdewynne, Báwdwyne, 277, 1606, 2384. (Cf. Br. p. 194).
Cáerlyone, 61.
Cálaburne, Cáliburne, Cályburne, 4193, 4230, 4242 (= *Excalybur*
    in Malory).

Cápados, 580 (= Cappadocia).

Chástelayne, Chásteleynne, 2952, 3028.   (In Malory Chestelayne).

Chrístofre, 2390.

Clárybalde, 2497.

Clárymownde, Cléremonde, 1603, 1638, 2497, 3635, 4265.   (In Malory Cleremond).

Cléremus, 1603, 1638.   (Cf. Br. p. 194).

Cónstantyne, 282.

Córdewa, 1866.

Dámyat, 578 (= Damietta).

Dánuby, 622.

Dólfinede, Dólfyne, Dólphyne, 2653, 2970, 3023 (= Dauphiné).

Élamet, 575.

Érmonye, 573.

Érmyngalle, 1825.

Éwandre, Éwandyre, Éwaynedyre, 1622, 1868, 1904.   (In Geoffr. of Monm. Evander. Cf. Br. p. 224).

Éwfrates, 574.

Fámacoste, 2761 (= Famagosta).

Flóridas, fflóridas, Flórydas, 2490, 2755, 2778, 2803, 3018, 3112.

Gálele, 592.

Gályrane, 3636.

Gáryere, 592.

Gólapas, 2124.

Gólyas, 3419 (= Goliath).

Hérygalle, 1742.   (Cf. Br. p. 194).

Híllary, 625.

Iénitalle, 2112.

Ióatalle, 2889.

Iólyan, 2889.

Iósephate, 2876.

Iúlius, Iúlyus, 115, 2877, 3410.   ·

Káelyone, Kárlyone, 3512, 3916.   (Cf. Cáerlyone, above).

Károlus, 3423.

Lúcius, Lúcyus, 23, 128, 251, 383, 419, 460.   (Cf. Br. p. 182).

Lúmbarddye, Lúmbardye, Lúmberddye, Lúmberdye, 135, 350, 429, 498, 1972, 2406, 2654, 2997, 3108, 3585, 3594.

Lýonelle, 1516, 2227, 3637, 4266.

Mácedone, 603.

Mákabee, 3413.

Málebranche, 4062, 4174.

Méneduke, 1919, 4077, 4267.

Názarethe, 591.

Nórmaundye, 44.

Pórtyngale, 1028.

Príamous, Príamus, Prýamous, 2595, 2646, 2690, 2698, 2811, 2836, 2916, 4344.

Sárazene, Sárazenes, Sárzanez, Sárzynes, 599, 607, 624, 1626, 1846, 1854, 1911, 1960, 2277.

Sátanase, 3812.

Ségramoure, 1871. (In Malory *Sagramour le desyrus*).

Séxtenour, Séxtynour, 1625, 1700. (Cf. Br. p. 195).

Spányolis, 3700, (= *Espagnols*).

Súrgenale, 3532.

Vályant, 1982, 2064.

Vértennone, 3169.

Vríene, Vrýence, 337, 2066. (So also in Malory.)

c) in *Piers the Plowman:*

Absolon, C 4, 411.

Álberdus, A 11, 157 (= *Albertus*).

Ámalec, Amalek, A 3, 247; C 4, 422.

Ántony, B 15, 278.

Ástaroth, B 18, 402.

Áuynete, B 12, 257. (Cf. Skeat, vol. II, p. 186).

Áuynoun, B 19, 240 (= *Avignon*).

Bédleem, Béthleem, Béthlem, A 6, 18; B 12, 150; B 15, 538; B 17, 122; B 18, 233; B 19, 67.

Bélial, C 21, 284; C 23, 79.

Cálabre, B 6, 272.

Cáluarie, Cáluarye, C, 7, 319; B 11, 194; B 16, 164; B 19, 138.

Cléophas, B 11, 227.

Dóminik, B 15, 213.

Égydie, B 15, 274 (= *St. Egidius*).

Élyes, B 14, 65 (= *Elias*).

Érmonye, B 5, 535; B 15, 549 (= *Armenia*).

Érseny, C 18, 12 (= *St. Arsenius*).

Gálile, B 19, 143, 153.

Lóngeus, B 18, 79 (= *Longinus*).

Lúcifer, Lúcyfer, A 1, 39, 109, 114; C 3, 107; B 5, 502; C 6, 188;
C 7, 330; C 8, 116, 117; B 10, 419; B 12, 41; B 17, 8; B 18,
34, 137, 260, 270, 308, 314, 346, 400; B 19, 55.

Mágdaleigne, Máudeleyn, A 11, 279; B 13, 194.

Mákamede, Mákemede, Mákomet, Mákometh, B 3, 327; A 4, 37;
B 15, 391; B 18, 159, 165, 239, 314. (Cf. *Máhon* above).

Názareth, Názereth, B 15, 486; B 19, 133.

Néptalim, Néptalym, B 15, 486; C 18, 261.

Rósamounde, B 12, 48.

Sálamon, A 3, 84; B 3, 330; C 9, 243; B 10, 450; A 11, 257;
B 12, 42, 269; C 14, 198.

Séneca, B 14, 304.

Tróianus, B 11, 136, 153; B 12, 210, 280 (= *Trajanus*).

Ýpocras, B 12, 44 (= *Hippocrates*).

Ýsodore, B 15, 37 (= *St. Isodore*).

Zácheus, B 13, 195.

2 b. Proper Names of three Syllables with stress on the second Syllable.

a) in the *Troy-Book*:

Achílles, 3651, 4487, 4513, 5190.

Adásthon, 5438 (= *Adrastus*).

Agéstra, 5516.

Agrésta, 6199.

Alcánus, 6543.

Alména, 292 (= *Alcmena*).

Amphénor, 7705. (In Guido *Alpinor*).

Amphímac, Amphímacus, Amphímakus, Amphímas, Amphýmake,
6377, 11287, 11354, 11599, 11611.

Anchíses, 12900.

Anténor, 1859.

Antíssas, 12444.

Appóllo, Appóllus, 4266, 4274, 8137.

Ascátus, Askáthes, 13397, 13431, 13434 (= *Acastus*. Cf. *Aschatus*
above).

Assándra, 13479.

Assándrus, 12781, 12784.

Enéus, 6380. (In Guido *Heneus*).

Eufórmus, 6858 (= *Euphorbus*).
Evfráton, 5495 (= *Euphrates*).
Vlýxes, 13106.

b) in *Piers the Plowman*:
Abráam, C 14, 5.

3a. Proper Names of four or more Syllables with stress on the first Syllable.

a) in the *Troy-Book*:
Ágamynon, 7688, 8919, 9381.
Álexaunder, Álexsaunder, Alisaunder, 314, 1479, 7562.
Ánchinordes, 1559. (In Guido *Antonorides*).
Árchelaus, Árchillaus, 5570, 7688.
Árchillacus, 5512.
Árchisalus, 4062 (= *Arcesilaus*).
Ardelaus, 6159. (So also in Guido).
Ástionac, 8483 (= *Astyanax*).
Édiana, 4275. (In Guido *Diana*).
Éxiona, 1387 (= *Hesione*).

b) in the *Morte Arthure*:
Ámbyganye, 572.
Íberius, 86. (Cf. Br. p. 182).

c) in *Piers the Plowman*:
Álisaundre, B 6, 535; B 12, 45; B 15, 549.
Árestotle, Áristotle, A 11, 130; B 12, 44; C 12, 216; C 15, 194.
Iérusalem, Ihérusalem, B 17, 51; B 18, 17.
Nábugodonosor, A 8. 139.
Róchemadore, B 12, 37. (Cf. Skeat vol. II, p. 179).
Sámaritan, B 17, 48, 63, 297; C 20, 106.
Thólomeus, C 13, 175 (= *Ptolemy*).

3b. Proper Names of four or more Syllables with stress on the second Syllable.

a) in the *Troy-Book*:
Agámenon, Agámynon, 2824, 3576, 3644, 3668, 3741, 4789, 4819, 9384.

Andrómaca, 8425.
Archílacus, 6101 (= Archilochus).
Athólapo, 6330 (= Ascalaphus).
Elíatus, 1282 (= Alyattes).
Epístafus, Epístaphus, 5525, 7647.
Ermónia, 2833 (= Hermione).
Eufémius, Euphýmus, 6221 (= Euphemus).
Exíona, Exína, 1724, 1762, 2171, 3140, 4889, 7080 (= Hesionc).
Idýmynus, Ydímius, 6461, 12762 (= Idomeneus).

b) in Piers the Plowman:
Iherúsalem, B 17, 19.

3c. Proper Names of four or more Syllables with stress on the third syllable.

a) in the Troy-Book:
Archeláus, 6335.
Colofáges, 13154 (= Lotophagi).
Ethimýssa, 12445.

b) in Piers the Plowman:
Arestótle, B 12, 266.

Among the proper names of three or more syllables we may distinguish 1. Those that have the classical form and stress, e. g. Achílles, Anténor, Anchíses, Archeláus. 2. Those that have the classical form, but Germanic accent, e. g. Achilles, Cássandra, Médea, Mínerva. 3. Those that show a popularised or mutilated form with classical accent, e. g. Alména, Amphímak, Ascátus, Evfráton. 4. Those that show a popularised, mutilated, or shortened form and Germanic accent, e. g. Clúnestra, Díomed, Lýcomede, Ámphimak.

The majority of the names of classical derivation have the Germanic accent. In those of three syllables and beginning with vowels, the stress is more frequently on the second than on the first syllable. Such names, when consisting of four or more syllables, have the accent as often on the first as on the second syllable. From the nature of the subject, the names in the Troy-Book are of classical origin. In the Morte Arthure they are chiefly of Romance or Celtic derivation, and those of three or more syllables are all accented on the first.

The prevalence of Germanic accentuation in our proper names arises from various causes. In the first place, our alliterative poets probably possessed only an imperfect knowledge of the classical forms and the correct pronunciation of the proper names. They derived their knowledge of them from the Mediæval Latin sources that supplied the material for their own works. Hence, they would adopt an accentuation most in accordance with the stress prevailing in English words, and with the exigencies of the alliteration, while mutilated forms might occasionally creep in through the carelessness of the scribes.

These remarks apply not only to the classical names of the *Troy-Book*, but equally to those of Romance or Celtic origin in the *Morte Arthure*. Whereas in the learned Chaucer a strong French influence shows itself in the accentuation of proper names, the less cultured alliterative poets here also adopted or followed the Germanic stress. In Chaucer the nature of his rhythm produced considerable variety of accentuation, often in the same word. (Cf. ten Brink § 294). The alliterative poet usually made the first letter of the first syllable serve for the alliteration. Yet accentuations like *Áchilles*, &c., found both in Chaucer and in our alliterative poets, would seem to show that they must at least have been familiar to the writers, as well as the classical stress. In Mod. E. also we have forms and accentuations like *Hómer, Óvid, Hórace, Sállust, Vírgil*, &c.

Index of Words.

In the following Index, words quoted from Middle English texts, and Middle English words from other sources (dictionaries, vocabularies, etc.), are printed in „spaced" type. Different forms of the same word are given only when identity of meaning is not obvious. Abbreviations are: *n.* = *noun*, *adj.* = *adjective*, *adv.* = *adverb*, *v.* = *verb*, *O.* = *Old*, *D.* = *Dutch*, *E.* = *English*, *F.* = *French*, *HG.* = *High German*. The references are to the pages.

abaiste, 105.
abated, 84, 87, 88.
abase, 105.
abash, 84, 86, 87, 105.
abedde, 27.
abide, 32, 40.
abilite, 73, 120.
abite, 34.
ablamed, 34.
ablyndeth, 34.
a-bostede, 34.
abouenn, 27, 27.
abouȝt, 34.
about, 26.
aboute, 25, 26, 44, 45, 51.
above, 30.
abrode, 27, 34.
abrybeth, 34.
absence, 63.
absens, 59, 62, 63, 108, 110.
absent (*v.*), 98, 99, 125.
absolucion, 70, 114, 117.
absolven, 114, 117.
absteyne, 84.
academy, 75.
acatalepsy, 71.
accent (*v.*), 98, 125.
accept, 84.

access(e), 63, 108, 113.
accesse, 60, 108, 110, 113.
accessory, 83, 118.
accidie, 77.
accorde (*v.*), 86, 87, 114.
accounted, 84, 86, 87, 89.
a-cloye, 106.
acombre, 107.
acordaunce, 67, 114.
a-corse, 34.
acouped, 106.
across, 31.
adequacy, 118.
admirable, 118.
adolescence, 71.
adorably, 83.
adoune, 27, 46.
adradde, 34.
adreynt, 34.
adulator, 71.
adulatory, 83.
advertise, 103, 125.
advisedly, 81.
advisement, 77.
afaiten, 106.
a-ferd, 34.
afferes (*n.*), 60, 108, 110.
affermyt, 84.

affiaunce, 67, 115, 116.
afforce (*v.*), 104.
afforse (*adv.*), 82, 124.
affray (*n.*), 76, 109.
affray (*v.*), 104, 105, 109.
affrayned, 34.
a-fote, 27.
afrontede, 87.
after, 48, 51.
afterwarde, 7, 14, 19, 107.
afurst, 27.
afyngred, 27.
against, 27, 30, 50.
a-gast, 34.
agayne, 27.
agaynes, 50.
aggravate (*v.*), 125.
aggregate (*v.*), 125.
a-glotye, 34.
ago(o), 39.
ago, 40.
agon, 34.
agreued, 89.
aionet, 84.
aiugget, 84, 86.
ajournede, 86.
alarme (*n.*), 60, 108.
alayed, 87.
albificacioun, 117.
alchemy, 77.
alconomye, 77, 121.
alkin, 21.
all, 21, 31.
allocate, 125.
allowance, 67, 114.
almaries, 77, 120.
aloft, 27.
alose, 106.
alouer, 31.
alowe, 86, 87, 114.
also, 22.
alternate (*adj.*), 83, 123.
alternation, 75.
althing, 21.
alway, 22.
always, 22.
a-lyghte, 34.

a-maysterd, 107.
ambages, 75.
ambry, 77.
ambush, 105.
amende, 87.
amirous, 80, 123.
ammoniac, 83, 124.
among, 26, 30.
amonge(s), 25, 26, 30.
amongst, 26, 27.
amorous, 80.
amortesed, 102.
amounteth, 87.
ampolles, 77.
a-mydde, 27.
anabasis, 71.
analogical, 83.
ancestres, 72.
ancestry, 71.
anecdote, 71.
animall, 75.
anoisyt, 104.
anoyeddyde, 86, 89.
anoyntide, 84.
anuyed, 87.
any wise, 21.
apaied, 106.
aparail (*n.*), 67, 115, 116.
aparte (*adv.*), 82, 124.
apas (*adv.*), 81, 124.
apeel (*n.*), 60, 108, 110.
apendeth, 87.
apogee, 71.
a-pose, 106.
apoysende, 107.
appanage, 71.
apparant, 80, 82, 123.
appareld, 101, 102.
appelé (*F.*), 111.
appere, 85, 87.
apperte(ly), 81, 82, 123.
apply, 99, 125.
apprentice, 111.
approche, 85, 86, 87.
appurtenaunce, 66, 118.
aquencheth, 34.
aquests, 63, 108.

confus (*adj.*), 79, 82, 115, 123.
confusede, 93, 125.
confusion, 68, 113, 115, 117.
congeyde, 105, 125.
coniuracioun, 68, 113, 117.
coniured, 95, 125.
conjoin, 99, 125.
connse, 98, 104, 105, 106, 114, 125, 129.
conquerid, 86, 125.
consayuit, 85, 90, 95, 125.
conscience (*F.*), 17.
conseilleth, 88, 89, 93, 125.
consent (*v.*), 99, 125.
consenteth, 95, 99, 125.
consequence, 71.
conseruatours, 65, 114, 118.
conservation, 71, 118.
conservator, 71.
conserven, 114.
consider, 102, 125.
consideration, 118.
consistorie, 66, 115, 116.
consistory, 117.
consolatory, 83.
conspire, 95, 125.
constable, 72, 120.
constellacion, 70, 113, 117.
constellated, 103, 125.
conster, 95.
constreyne, 95, 125.
construe, 95, 98, 125, 129.
consuetude, 72.
consult (*n.*), 63, 108, 113.
consummate, 83, 123.
consume, 90.
consumet, 90, 98, 125.
contek (*n.*), 59, 107, 108, 110.
contemplacion, 70, 117.
contemplate, 103.
contenaunce, 66, 116.
contentions, 117.
conterfeteth, 101, 125.
conterroller, 67, 114.
contiguous, 83.
continuator, 72.
contour, 63, 108, 113.

contract (*n.*), 63, 108, 113.
contract (*v.*), 99, 125.
contrary, 80, 123.
contrary, 83, 116, 124.
contrast (*n.*), 63, 108, 113.
contreenede, 95, 125.
contreplede, 106, 125.
contricion, 70, 117.
contrite, 83, 123.
contrive, 95, 96.
controlen, 114.
contynu (*v.*), 102, 125.
contynually, 78.
connaye, 93, 125.
conuerted, 96, 125.
conventicle, 71, 72, 118.
converse (*n.*), 63.
conversely, 84.
convert (*v.*), 96.
conwayance, 116.
conysaunce, 66, 116.
co-operation, 71.
cope-borde, 9.
corage, 64.
corageous, 79, 124.
corectoures, 70, 98, 114, 115, 116.
coriander, 75.
coroner, 130.
coronyd, 104, 130.
corrette (*v.*), 98, 114, 125, 129.
corridor, 75.
corrosive, 83, 116, 123, 124.
corrupt (*adj.*), 68, 115.
corupcioun, 68, 70, 113, 115, 117.
cosmeticks, 75.
coueite, 99, 130.
couenable, 78, 124.
couenant, 65, 66, 115, 116.
couetous, 78.
counge, 59.
counter-mand, 103, 125.
countersign (*v.*), 125.
countresegge, 107, 125.
couytise, 77, 120.
coveitier (*OF.*), 130.
cravat, 65, 122.
crosse-dayes, 9.

recorde (*n.*), 60, 109, 110.
recorded, 97, 128.
recorder, 97.
recounseld, 102, 128.
recover, 102.
recrayed, 105, 128.
recreaunt, 81, 82, 123.
recusants, 72.
redolent, 83, 123.
redoundet, 86.
redresse (*n.*), 58, 109, 110.
reffourmed, 98, 128.
reflex (*adj. & n.*), 84, 123.
refractory, 83.
refresshe, 86.
refuse (*v.*), 97, 128.
refuse (*v.*), 97.
refut, 86.
regratour, 78, 119.
rehearse, 94.
reherse, 89, 94, 97, 98, 128.
rehetede, 104, 128.
reioyse, 97, 128.
rekeuered, 101, 128.
relacion, 70, 117.
relatif, 79.
relaxation, 71.
relayes (*v.*), 105, 128.
reles (*n.*), 62, 109, 110.
releshe, 92, 128.
releue, 97, 128.
religion, 70.
relikes, 57, 59, 107, 109, 110.
relish (*v.*), 128.
relyed, 87, 97, 128.
relygeous, 79.
remedie, 116.
remediless, 84, 124.
remedy (*n. & v.*), 124.
remembirde, 102, 114, 128.
remembraunce, 70, 114, 116.
remenaunt, 59, 109, 110.
remeve, 92, 94, 98, 128.
remission, 70, 117.
remove, 92.
renayede, 105.
render, 128.

renegade, 72.
reneye, 105, 128.
renonse, 93.
reno(u)n(e), 62, 109, 110.
renownde, 79.
repast (*n.*), 62, 109, 110.
rependez, 105, 128.
repent, 94, 97, 114, 128.
repentance, 69, 115.
repentaunse, 68, 69, 70, 113, 114, 116.
repentaunt, 68, 114.
repertory, 72.
repreff, 63, 109, 110.
reprehend, 103, 128.
repreuet, 86, 88, 98, 128.
reprobate, 71.
reprofe, 58, 109.
repugnet, 104, 106, 128.
requit, 94, 128.
resceyte (*n.*), 63, 109, 110.
rescow (*v.*), 86, 87, 128, 129.
rescowe (*n.*), 59, 109, 110.
rescue (*v.*), 128.
residu (*OF.*), 116.
residue, 66, 116.
resolvend, 72.
resort (*v.*), 86, 128.
resoun, 122.
ressort (*n.*), 63.
restitucioun, 70, 117.
restore, 86, 93, 128.
restreynede, 94, 128.
retain, 93.
retaynit, 93, 128.
retenaunce, 78, 120.
retenuz, 66.
reticence, 72.
retinue, 71, 72.
retournes (*v.*), 94, 138.
retrograde, 83, 123.
return (*v.*), 94.
reuenge (*v.*), 95, 128, 129.
reuerenced, 101, 128.
reuerssede, 95, 128.
reuertede, 95, 128.
reueste, 105, 128.

Lightning Source UK Ltd.
Milton Keynes UK
UKHW010214271118
332995UK00015B/1889/P